The Oxford College Barges

The Oxford College Barges

THEIR HISTORY AND ARCHITECTURE

Clare Sherriff

Unicorn Press
London

for John Wolstenholme and Norman Dix

Unicorn Press
76 Great Suffolk Street
London SE1 0BL

email: unicorn@tradford.demon.co.uk

Copyright © 2003 Clare Sherriff
Illustrations © the Copyright holders
as acknowledged with the reproductions

First published 2003 by Unicorn Press

All rights reserved. No part of this
publication may be reproduced, stored in
a retrieval system, or transmitted in any
form or by any means, electronic, mechanical,
photocopying, recording or otherwise, without
the prior permission of the publishers.

ISBN 0 906290 71 6

Designed and typeset by Ferdinand Pageworks
Printed in Great Britain

Contents

Preface	1
The Architect's Barges:	
A History of the Oxford College barges	3
Pre-History:	
The Thames Livery Company barges	7
The Prime Player:	
The OUBC	10
The University:	
Mid-Nineteenth to Mid-Twentieth-Century Barge Users	23
The Front Runners:	
The Colleges Who Purchased the Livery Barges:	
Oriel	27
Univ	36
Exeter	45
Balliol	47
Queen's	50

Contents

Brasenose	**55**
Christ Church	**57**
Pembroke	**59**
Worcester	**61**
New College	**61**
Corpus Christi	**65**
Jesus	**72**
Magdalen	**76**
Trinity	**80**
St John's	**83**
Wadham	**85**
St Edmund Hall	**87**
Keble	**88**
Lincoln	**92**
Hertford	**93**
Merton	**97**
Other Barges	100
Transported Meanings	102
Chronological Table	108
Sources	110
Footnotes	111

Preface

In writing this history I am aware of the errors I will undoubtedly have made; new information and varied opinions continually alter any perspective. My knowledge of marine architecture is to say the least negligible, as is my understanding of the Oxford way of life. However in compiling a history of the barges based primarily on the archival evidence of the colleges, which I believe has never been done before in its entirety, an attempt has been made to group and compare them.

There are various highlights: Balliol's meticulous book-keeping and the Captain's comments on rowers' performance:

> Bow was a stiff back stylist from Shrewsbury and two a tortuous elder predestined for the Church.

And of the Eight of 1937

> No 2 a very deceptive OUDS man looks rather a pansy;
> No 4 a huge Etonian of casual temperament;
> No 7 a rangy Australian – queer to look at but a damned sound oar.

More relevant to the barges are the OUBC ledgers, complete with a collection of original bills dating back to the 1850s, with the transactions of that first 'pleasure barge' recorded. University College's rich photographic collection of the barges and contemporary rowing dress along with Corpus Christi's pencil drawing, believed partly to be in the hand of the Victorian architect, T.G. Jackson (1835-1924) are notable inclusions. Jackson's drawings for the Oriel barge (Royal Academy of Arts) are unique to the history of the college barges. John Oldrid Scott (1841-1913) was among other architects and builders who contributed to the design of the barges.

Essential to the writing of this book have been the people connected with the barges: old members, boating people and rowers whose enthusiasm has been extraordinarily helpful, most notably John Wolstenholme (University College, 1956-59). Norman Dix, the Univ boatman's contribution has been of a star-like quality; his information has been the underlying first-hand experience that I have called on time and time again. I am particularly grateful to Richard Norton, Chairman of the Trust for the Preservation of the Oxford College Barges for his advice, numerous corrections and patient proof-reading and to all the college archivists who have answered my questions. Steve Royle of the OUBC has been exemplary in his donation of time and help. Essentially, I owe my inspiration to my husband's constantly roving eye, which brought the University College (Univ) barge into our lives.

'University College State Barge Oxford, 1880', *The Building News*

The Architects' Barges

A History of the Oxford College Barges

In the twenty-first century the very idea of an Oxford college barge awakens an incredulous questioning that such extravagant vessels were used simply as clubhouses for nineteenth-century Oxford students on the river. This perspective aims to question why such waterborne artifice appealed to the colleges. In doing so it attempts to chart the history of the barges, beginning with their pre-history in the City of London livery barges. It examines the roles of the players, the prime initiators, the OUBC (Oxford University Boat Club), the colleges who followed suit, the 'users', students, dons and coaches and the 'doers', i.e. those that made and maintained such infrastructure for the colleges. Individual college records, Boat Club Accounts and Captain's Books are the primary sources, alongside oral evidence. The perspective is that of an enthusiast, but not an Oxford one. Being fully aware of the elitist nature of the enquiry it seeks to redress the balance with a view of life from the 'other' side of the barges, in particular where possible that of the college boatmen, the 'Bargemasters' in their own right.[1]

The barges themselves are treated chronologically and examined thematically in terms of architectural style: the two stylistic giants the Gothic and the Classical, with variations of Edwardian Baroque, Arts and Crafts and Art Nouveau, represent the styles commissioned from an interesting collection of architects employed by the colleges. Economics, although restricted within the boundaries of Boat Club Accounts, was seemingly not an essential problem to the early life of the barges, any difficulties being surmounted by energetic fund raising exercises.

It is believed that ten barges are still in existence today, of the supposed twenty-five originals[2]; these are waterborne largely due to the efforts of a second generation of 'players', a mixture of romantic and realist, who have transported these vessels into their post-modern roles.[3] An examination of these characters and barges proves the hypothesis that the Oxford barges are a true, if somewhat frail metamorphosis of a tradition derived from the fifteenth-century livery company ceremonial vessels. This in itself draws reference to the Venetian state barges and the even earlier Roman and Viking craft. Contingent forces conspired in the mid-nineteenth century to reform them into university clubhouses. Later metamorphoses included house boats, conference centres, restaurants and pleasure palaces. The age-old adage 'Form follows function' is somewhat negated by new uses.

In the late nineteenth and twentieth century the barges were moored alongside Christ Church Meadow on the Thames (or Isis as the river is called at Oxford), protected by a row of railings erected by Christ Church, who own the

The barges at Christ Church Meadows, c. 1870
By kind permission of the Centre for Oxfordshire Studies

From left to right the Salter's (unconfirmed), the OUBC, Brasenose, Exeter, Univ, Christ Church, Oriel and Queen's barges.

meadow. Each college paid rental for a gate protecting their barge; this was kept padlocked all the time when not in use and fines were incurred should it be left open. All the barges had a ferry punt, licensed to carry twelve people and a set of steps for ascending to the towpath. Most had a 40' raft attached to the barge from which to boat.

Max Beerbohm's novelette *Zuleika Dobson* weaves a fantasy love affair around the phenomenon of the Oxford barges at

One of Osbert Lancaster's illustrations for Max Beerbohm's *Zuleika Dobson*
Courtesy of the Randolph Hotel and Macdonald Hotels (UK) Limited

Summer Eights Week; it describes the milieu of raft and punt, bringing the scene to life:

> standing on the edge of the raft that makes a floating platform for the barge, William, the hoary bargee, was pushing them off with his boat-hook, wishing them [the crew] luck with deferential familiarity [4]
>
> from all the barges the usual punt-loads of young men were being ferried across to the towing-path – young men naked of knee, armed with rattles, post-horns, motor-hooters, gongs and other instruments of clangour [5]

By the late nineteenth century, most barges had a boatman whose job it was to look after the workings of the craft. He had to ensure it had fresh water and also that the bilges were pumped out; this was a regular occurrence. Adequate heating was needed in the winter; additionally he was responsible for blades (oars), boats and the young men who were learning to row. These boatmen were fathers of their respective boatclubs and played an integral role in the students' rowing life; the barge was the 'boatclub's home'. Friendships were established from the barges that would be life-long. The barges were part of Oxford's way of life at the time. H.G. Wells' *The New Machiavielli* describes the MP Richard Remington in Oxford: 'We went down Carfax I remember to Folly Bridge and inspected the barges'.[6] The barges lay in a specific order and during Eights Week were often tied to piles and tree trunks; this was to prevent them keeling over with the weight of supporters on the upper deck who often moved en masse to get a better view of the racing. Few who have lived in Oxford or walked the tow path during those years can fail to remember, or been uplifted by the line up of these waterborne giants sitting quietly on the bank of the river, flags flying, windows open, a hive of rowing activity emanating from their decks. They were to prove an inspiration to oarsmen and artists alike.

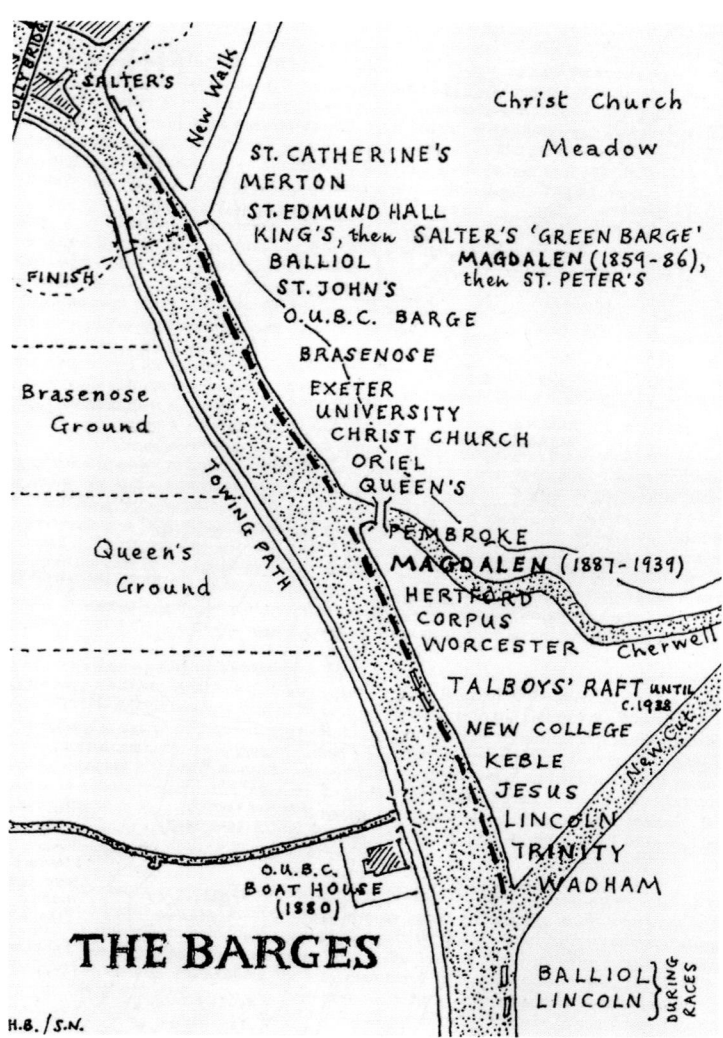

Map drawn by Stella Newton based on OUBC Eights Programme, 1935.
By kind permission of Peter Fullerton, Magdalen College.

Pre-History

THE THAMES LIVERY COMPANY BARGES

Anne Petrides's *State Barges on the Thames* provides a pictorial explanation of the early livery barges. Water carriage was from early times a principal method of transport in and around the City of London. Most royal or state processions, Petrides writes, were by river, emanating from the various palaces scattered along the Thames: including Greenwich, Whitehall and Hampton Court.[7] The livery companies, early trading societies modelled on the northern trading guilds of Antwerp, reflected this royal pomp and pageantry from the fifteenth century with their own barges. These grouped annually for the Lord Mayor's Procession, where they rowed in waterborne parade, in strictly hierarchical order, until 1856.[8]

Petrides explains that the barges were of 'wherry construction', being basically 'a vast rowing boat' with a 'house' on top decorated according to the aesthetic whims of the time.[9] T. Sayle's *The Barges of the Merchant Taylors' Company* suggests that prior to the seventeenth century the barge houses were smaller, probably with room for only six or seven people. Certainly by the eighteenth century they seemed to display structures which took up a good third of the hull, capable of housing a sizeable number.[10] Notable features often included a massive lute stern decorated with the arms of the company and a cornucopia of 'allegorical maritime figures'. The rowers (up to eighteen in number) sat forward, in front of the 'house' of the boat. The Skinners' barge of 1656 shows a multi-pillared two tiered temple-type edifice, followed by the stern section which housed the 'mynstrelsie' with seats for musicians with 'drummes, flutes and trumpets blohyng'[11] The Bargemaster steered from this lofty and seemingly noisy vantage point.[12] A Merchant Taylors' inventory of 1805 writes of 'eight cloaks, eight handsome fashionable musician's dress hats with feathers' being provided for the men of the barge; the Bargemaster and rowers themselves resplendent in their livery uniform.[13]

Architectural decoration in the form of pillars, porticoes, arabesque and foliate devices, cornices, architraves and various forms of inventive fenestration were common detailing. Gilded lions, fish, lambs, seahorses, shells, angels, mermaids, wyverns and dragons provided iconic reference to identify ownership of the various barges. Upper decks, as seen on the barge of the Worshipful Company of Fishmongers, *c.* 1773, were used with staircase access by the eighteenth century. The Merchant Taylors' barge of 1764 has 'a handsome portico before the house', 'thirty six sashes of the best plate' and 'two capitals of the Corinthian order', an order derived from the city of Corinth, being historically associated with luxury and feminity. Petrides writes that the lavishly-decorated Lord Mayor's or City barge of 1807 had 'two fluted columns on each side of the front door', and that it 'was made up of wainscot with mahogany frames to the windows'. The use of architectural decoration was therefore well established on the barges. In architectural terms it was a recognised language utilised to codify quality, prestige and meaning; it was therefore easily transferable to a temple-like structure on the water.

It was the last Merchant Taylors' barge of 1800 built by Richard Roberts of Lambeth, the Queen's Bargemaster, which was to be the flagship, chameleon and harbinger of change to Oxford. T. Sayle writes that Searle and Roberts, both Thames boat builders, declined to purchase the barge, but that it was initially bought by Wyld and Noulton for £63. By the end of 1846 it had been purchased by the inventive organisers of the OUBC, the newly-formed Oxford University Boat Club. They were to continue the tradition of club usage, water processions, music on board for ceremonial occasions but (perhaps fortuitously) not that of passing the

The Merchant Taylors' barge of 1800 photographed *c.* 1870s.

old barge to the Bargemaster. They too, like the liverymen of the Merchants Taylors' Company, were later to be worried about the 'danger of [the barge's] bottom coming out if squeezed in a crowd of other barges'.[14] A similar concern was the necessity to have to pay for 'watching the Barge 15 nightes', (the barges, sitting lonely on the water at night have, it seems, always been a target for pranks and vandalism). The prototype set 'sail' for Oxford taking with her a history of ceremonial usage and prestige, conveying such notions to a new riverside medium.[15]

It was therefore from the early livery barges that the model emerged for future generations of Oxford college barges. Design features which were utilised well into the twentieth century included a flat hull, with a draft of approximately 3', lengths varying from 60-90', upon which was placed a large 'house' structure' which was eventually to take up the greater part of the vessel. (The livery barges, as previously mentioned, had needed a considerable space forward for the rowers). The saloon of the Oxford college barges was the main living area where the blades were stored. It was normally heated by a fireplace. The area under the stern was often used for a stove heating water. The use of the sash window was a common feature and a row of twelve each side was not unusual.

Decoration was in the main classical, using pilasters, pediments, fluting, scrolling etc. but varied widely in order to identify and individualize. It was here that the alter ego of certain colleges could emerge, being a far cry from the more serious architecture of the college facades and quads. The use of an upper deck as a viewing platform was an essential feature taken from the livery barges, as were grand doorcases and entrances, often supported by columns. An entablature sporting the college arms, as opposed to livery insignia, was normally positioned to the fore of the craft. The great stern rise of the earlier barges, accommodating minstrel and bargemaster, gradually became redundant but many later designs still held the notion of the 'grand sweep'.

Norton writes that there were barges in use at Oxford before the livery barges arrived. He believes that the go-betweens, who suggested that the redundant livery barges would be of use to the Oxford colleges, were the boatmen King and Hall. It was an easy and inspired metamorphosis.

The Prime Player

THE OUBC

The Oxford University Boat Club was founded in 1839 with the aim of promoting the sport of rowing and encouraging the dexterity and athletic prowess of the early Victorians on the river.[16] Emphasis had shifted in Victorian times to physical exercise; the Georgians, in more leisurely fashion, had fenced, walked, danced and hunted. 1839 was the year that the first Henley Regatta was held and according to many marks the start of regulated competitive rowing at Oxford. The Reverend Sherwood in his seminal book, *Oxford Rowing*, writes that the first organised Oxford college boat race took place as early as 1829.[17] The Reverend Tuckwell's *Reminiscences of Oxford* suggests that before 1843 the college races were 'mere incident', but that it was the 1843 Henley race that truly boosted the enthusiasm for rowing at Oxford.[18] There are undoubtedly varied opinions but the general consensus seems to be that the early 1840s saw the birth of organised rowing at Oxford.

There are two primary sources available to historians of the OUBC, one being a complete set of Captain's Books dating from 1839-1954 held by the Bodleian Library.[19] These are essentially records of university racing; Torpids in the winter and Eights in the summer, the Sculls and Fours, all with accompanying critiques (dry witticism prevailed) of individual oarsmen, their characters and prowess. They include accounts of the Henley Regattas, college races, race charts, and of course, the Oxford and Cambridge Boat Race[20]. Secondly there is a copious collection of ledgers, complete with collections of original bills and notice books often relating to the OUBC barge, held by the OUBC archivist. The latter probably constitutes the most complete collection of material available on any one of the Oxford barges. Importantly, minutes of the 1839 inaugural meeting of the OUBC record that

a barge should be hired for the use of the club[21]

Leather bound OUBC account's ledgers starting in 1839 record a healthy opening receipt of £239 16s 6d, the first mention of a barge in the accounts being:

Loder for china for barge – 4s[22]

This suggests that catering was an early priority. A later entry 'Jack for Barge £10' probably confirms Sherwood's supposition that 'the first university barge was hired from a man named Heather for £10 a term'[23]. To date no picture or photograph confirms the design of this first barge, although it is likely it was a simple structure. Sherwood, the first published source for a history of the early barges, also writes that Heather received a salary of £2 5s a term; an entry 'The Barge Servant for £2' dated December 9th is probably the reference to which he alludes.[24] An entry in the Captain's Book describes how, on June 10 1839, 'the club barge was given up for accommodation of ladies introduced by members'. Included in the club rules were two references to the barge:

viii) That no member drefs in the barge
xx)   That no dogs be admitted into the club barge and that any member transgrefsing this Rule be fined two shillings and sixpence[25]

Sherwood was himself Treasurer of the OUBC and a meticulous book-keeper who knew, and luckily recorded the history of the barges, to a great extent from first hand recollection. References are extant to John Heather's rent for the barge from December 5th 1839 for the sum of £9 9s through to Easter 1846.[26] In 1844 'new matting' was put down; incidentals are listed, such as an entry dated simply 1845 for 'matches, tapers and 2 penknives'. The receipts are neatly, even somewhat obsessively folded and pasted into the leather bound volume. The *OUBC Notices Book* of the same period reveals probably one of the earliest Procession Night leaflets:

Later years show printed admission tickets to the 'top of the barge', the upper decks providing an excellent viewing platform.

The connection to the City livery companies is recorded in 1846, when the first OUBC receipt's book records the entry:

'to the purchase of a large pleasure barge lately belonging to the Merchant Taylors' Company – £180'

A further £20 was paid for cushions, curtains, awning and extras and a similar amount paid for 'men's wages, carriage to London and hire of horse for bringing the boat back along the tow-path to Oxford'. (The boatbuilder Isaac King's journey to London and expenses are mentioned; it appears he was acting on behalf of the OUBC). Interestingly too, in this first account, is an entry 'paid Mesfs. Norton & Wyld for boats bottom being drefsed and odd work done to outside £5 10.1d'. Messrs. Norton and Wyld are recorded as the original purchasers from the Merchant Taylors' Company; it may well be that they too were instrumental in approaching the OUBC.

Alongside this is Isaac King's receipt for the final £100 owing on the University Boat Club barge; he had earlier been paid £110 19s 2d in 1849, which included the initial payment of £125 and a full list of sundries.

This huge structure with thirteen round-headed windows, a giant stern sweep and upper-railed deck was to act as an important design influence and precedent for future college barge building.[28]

The account's ledger of 1839-75 records a bill for furniture for 'the new barge and for fitting of floor cloth'. Numerous references to incidentals are recorded throughout the year: May 7-20th saw an account to 'hire of band -£17- to play on the club's barge', a similar entry mentions '£1 each evening for twelve instruments to be played on the club barge' from 6–9pm in the evening. Blacking the stove, repairing blinds, the purchase of cups and Grant's 'care of the barge' (the latter being a recurring cost), were typical expenses. Isaac King's receipt is extant in the *Accounts Book* of 1841-59. It reads: 'three men two days each cleaning and varnishing the house part of the club barge – shutters [probably internal] with oak varnish'. Similarly the account for the somewhat gargantuan feat of 'getting boat out of water with screw jacks' and the subsequent fresh varnishing with 'rossin and tallow the boats bottom' are indicators of maintenance work required to keep such a vessel in order. In those days, King's men, were even provided with beer for 'men at work', at a cost of 8s 9d.

The accounts show that the club barge went to Henley in July 1849 where two men were employed at a cost of £26 10s. This set another precedent; in future years when colleges owned their own barge they too would tow their barges down to the Regatta, equip them with flowers, lobsters, strawberries and cream and entertain their guests most royally, often setting up special 'Henley Funds' in order to do so.

From the 1850s the bills appear to increase, or may well be more meticulously recorded; they create a fascinating picture of life on the barge. There are accounts through to 1853 for 'graining' a paint finish to simulate wood, varnishing, putting new floor to 'first of barges, driving piles for a stage for the barge [this was for the rowers to boat from] and to new window frames'. Henry Slatter provided paper, ink and periodicals. In terms of day-to-day maintenance, entries for mops and buckets and other sundries occur. There are accounts for jellies, beers, brandy, port and biscuits which, juxtaposed with the normal day-to-day expenses, indicate the somewhat heady consumption of the rowers.

Time progresses in the journals; the year 1854 is an important date in the history of the Oxford college barges. The OUBC commissioned E.G. Bruton, an Oxford city surveyor, to design their new barge, which was to be built by Daniel Downing of Pangbourne. His letter accepting the commission is dated 13th June 1854.[29]

The OUBC advertised in *Jackson's Oxford Journal* 'to receive tenders for building house for barge' and further advertising (according to the receipt) was put locally in the *Oxford Chronicle*, the *Berks and Bucks Gazette* and nationally in *Bells Life*, London.

Plans of the barge, signed by Daniel Downing, dated 1854, are in the OUBC archives. She had a massive length of 95' and draught of 3'. Six sets of tripartite Gothic windows with trefoil effect were intersected by pilasters. The upper deck balustrading appears to have trefoil and Gothic fret work; benches and a full length canopy being provided for the comfort of the viewers. The music stands of the band were clearly visible to the stern. Two minute eye-like triangular windows were positioned to the upper section of the stern, creating a somewhat prehistoric whale-like image to this section of the barge.

The OUBC stipulated that Downing's work in building the hull was 'to be performed in the most efficient and workmanlike manner of the best materials in the respective kinds – the bottom is to be of the best seasoned 'Dantzie plank'.'

Easter 1854, in the accounts ledger, marks the first payment to Bruton of £10 for his designs and two payments to Downing of £100. A copy of the agreement between Downing and the OUBC is dated 1st September 1854. In this Downing agrees 'according to the best of his skill and knowledge to erect, build and completely finish the hull of a Barge (exclusive of the floor thereof) to the satisfaction of Edward George Bruton of Oxford, (Surveyor), for the sum of £299 to be paid over three instalments'. Receipted copies of both Downing's and Bruton's bills exist, Bruton's stating 'on account of my commission for superintending the erection of the new University Barge.'

Notices dated November 1854 state, 'that the University Barge [the old Merchant Taylors' barge] be disposed of'. These were placed in the *Oxford Chronicle* alongside the *Berks and Bucks Gazette*. In a letter concluding this deal, signed by W. Hall, the boatbuilder, dated December 11th 1854, he writes that 'I hereby agree to give the sum of £42 for the University Barge as advertised in the *Oxford Journal*'; John Bossom, another boat-builder, had bid £35.[30] It appears the Merchant Taylors' barge went first to Hall and later on to University College. B. Atkins sent a bill in 1855 'for removing goods from the old barge' (7s 6d). Slight confusion enters

Opposite: The Merchant Taylors' barge with the Univ VIII of 1862.
By kind permission of the Masters and Fellows of University College, Oxford

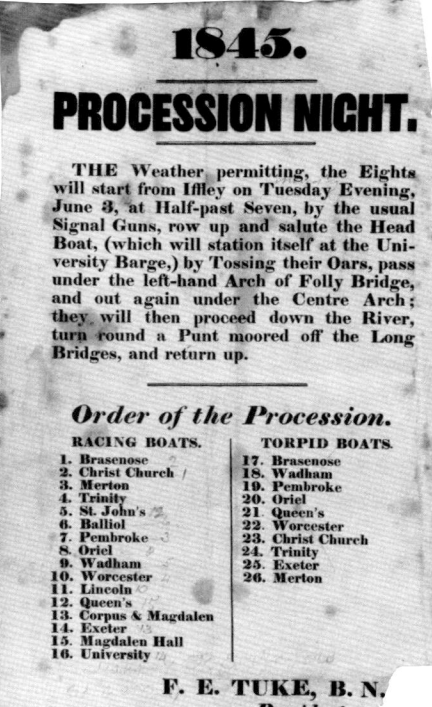

1845 Procession Night[27]

By kind permission of the OUBC

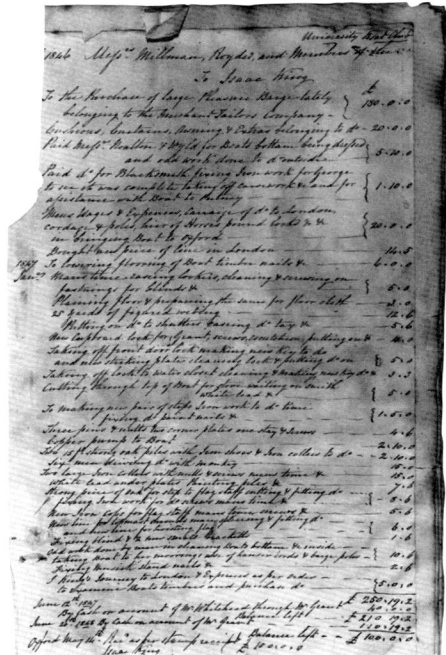

1846 'To the Purchase of large Pleasure Barge'

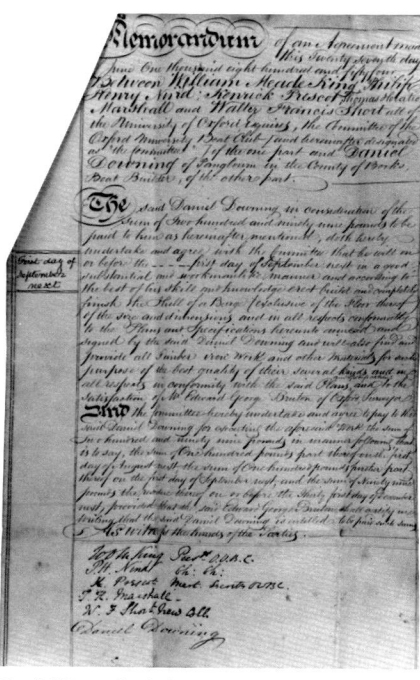

Daniel Downing's letter accepting commission of the Third OUBC barge

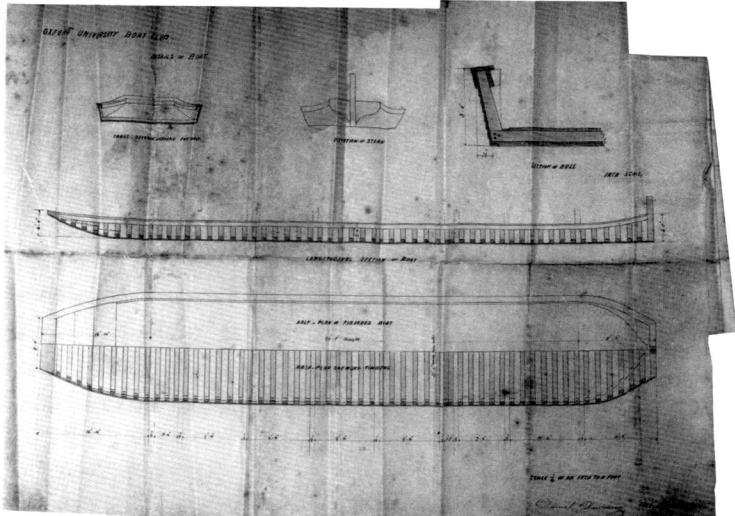

Daniel Downing's plans dated July 1st 1854

with a letter, dated November 13th 1854, signed by Bruton which certifies that Mr John Garth is entitled to an instalment of £300 upon account for building the new barge for the Oxford University Boat Club'. It is possible that he built the superstructure, which is recorded as having been built at Oxford, and Downing the hull.

However an entry in 1855 shows John Castle's builder's account for 'building new house on barge' as per estimate of £497. This makes detailed references to oak, deal and 'best strong patent glass' and even mentions the repairing and fixing of music stools on the barge. The total work took fifty-two-and-a-half days men's labour and approximately ninety-two days for a 'lad', reaching a healthy excess to the original estimate of £809 17s 9d.

On a more luxurious note, barge accoutrements include 'three marble cabinet washstands' from Spiers, 'four long paper knives with strong handles engraved with the letters OUBC' and a dozen blocks of almond soap. A grand idea of the interior embellishment can be gleaned from an account of 1855. This details velvet seating, rich carpet, blue tasselled blinds, the aforementioned marble washstands, oak magazine racks, Windsor chairs and a good-sized table to sit around, evoking the interior of a gentleman's club rather more than a rowing clubhouse.

> for making seats for club and committee room covering with superfine velvet, roller blinds, blue, mounted in blue merino blue tassells
> 42' of the best breufsells carpet making down in the dressing and committee room
> 90' of superior matting (bound with leather)
> polishing 12 windsor chairs from the old boat
> oak desk
> cloth for tables (bound with imperial lace)
> 3 muslin curtains for dressing room
> 4 looking glasses with solid oak frames
> oak frames for rules and banner
> oak letter box with glass panels
> floor cloth for water closets
> oak stand for *Bells Life* and newspapers

A carved marble clock case and movement was added later. A 'blue silk flag' flew from the flagstaff declaring the OUBC barge as centre stage to Oxford rowing.

Such expenditure dented a sizeable hole in the OUBC accounts. The year 1855 witnessed a mortgage agreement between T. Pilkington and the OUBC for £800 (a commission being paid to Mr Davenport of eleven guineas for the arrangement). Repayment of interest began at a rate of £45 but thereafter payments between £20–£26 were made half yearly from Michaelmas term 1855 to Easter 1870, along with various capital repayments. By 1871 the loan appears to have dropped to £350 and was now with the 'Old Bank'. Sherwood's *Treasurer's Private Book* clearly explains the mathematics behind this. The barge was mortgaged in 1855 for £800, £100 was paid in 1857, and £200 in 1858. By 1870 the old mortgage was paid off, the OUBC had inevitably grown weary of being charged interest on the full amount, despite having made deductions in the capital sum, and £500 borrowed from Old Bank who mortgaged the barge in 1870.

In this twenty-year period general maintenance expenses pursued their relentless path. Such entries varied from the delights of silk hats purchased from Thomas Randall in 1855 (the eights rowed in top hats) to a new white duck awning in 1859 (66'4" x 20') to cover the upper deck. Hall's 'cleaning scraping and pitching the University Barge' (1855) women cleaning, the breaking of ice and 'men at the gate during the college races' were other incidentals. Poor 'Charles Bofsom' was paid £35 in December 1858 'for cleansing the river underneath the University Barge', a seemingly impossible

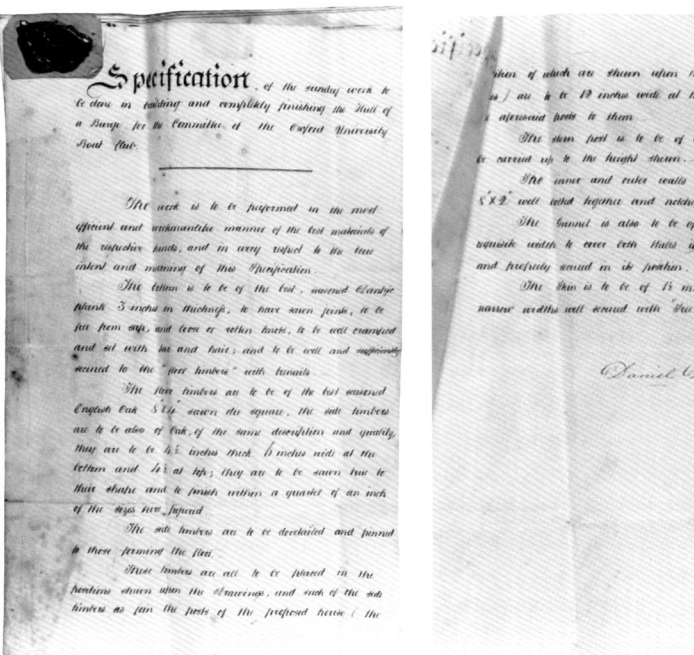

The OUBC specification

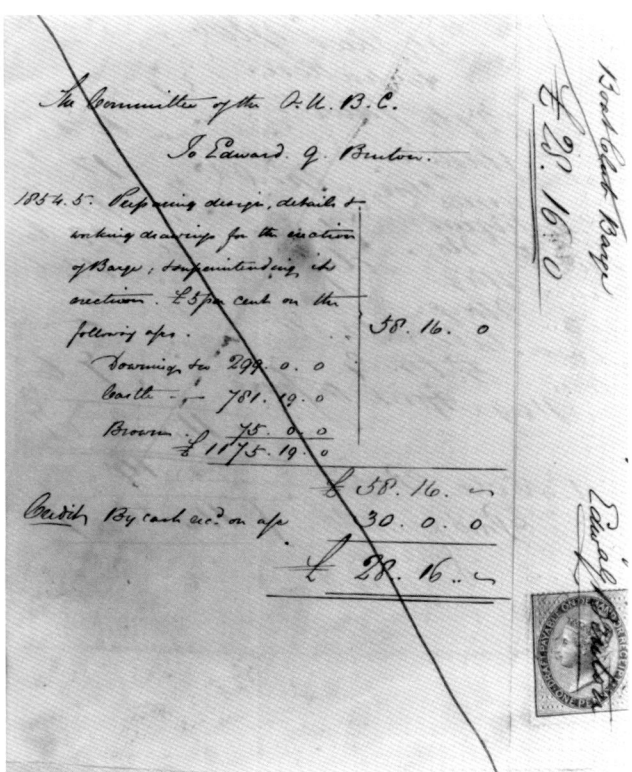

Downing and Bruton's bills for the University barge

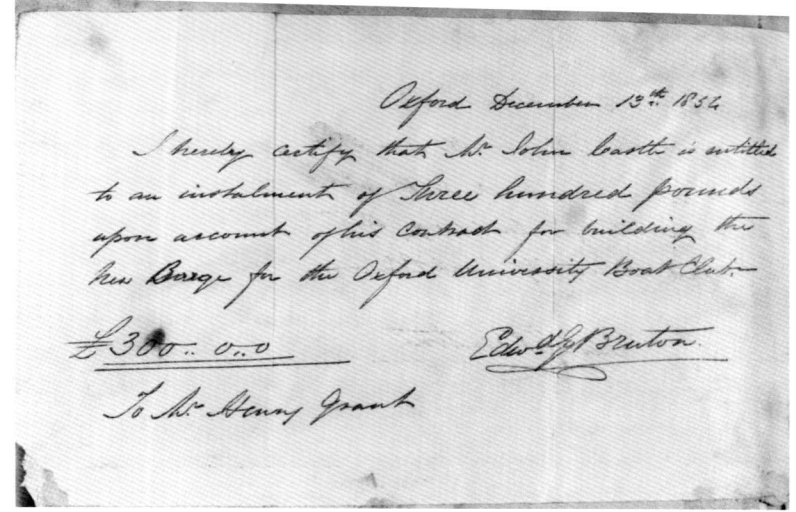

Bruton's letter of November 13th 1854

By kind permission of the OUBC

The Bruton 'Gothic' OUBC barge, 1871
By kind permission of the Master and Fellows of University College, Oxford

job. Weed removal around the barge, candles, horse hire, lead to the roof, coals, wines, spirits, fire insurance of £1 18s 6d (paid in 1863) constitute further entries. Constant stationery bills (the barge was well stocked with most periodicals and newspapers) postage stamps (all letters sent from the barge were stamped free of charge) even down to a clothes-horse in 1872, show fascinating minutiae. Decorative additions to the interior included Plowman's 'strong wrought iron Gothic fire-grate and an ornamental hot air stove' (a 'Gothic' chimney is clearly visible in the picture of the barge). In 1860 Roberts of Oxford were paid three guineas for 'engraving chair in Barge', which is most probably the Captains Chair still in existence today. Sherwood writes that £400 was spent on barge repairs and repainting in 1868 alone.

A great red leather-bound volume marked simply *OUBC* dated 1876-1893, protects Sherwood's meticulous book-keeping, with an accompanying volume working in parallel, dated June 1876 to November 1888, in which the bills are neatly folded and glued onto the pages, all tightly bound by a strong leather strap. The bills themselves, often beautifully engraved with trade insignia and written in copperplate, make fascinating reading; they comprehensively provide an account of local tradesmen and suppliers of stock needed to maintain the lifestyle of the OUBC barge during the mid- to late-nineteenth century. After 1878 the barge costs were entered under a separate heading, as were the boat race expenses, prior to this there had been no categorisation.

These accounts vary from William Bossom's looped and somewhat shaky hand for his work of raft building, piling to the barge and Tims' general maintenance for boats and as supplier of parts (in 1878 he helped with a leak on the barge).

Mrs Tims appears to be the chief towel washer of the period, submitting termly accounts. Rowing boats came from Salter's and Plummers provided cordage, light ropes etc. The occasional bill slipped in from T.G. Tagg, a well known boating name of East Molesley, Edward Ayling 'mast and scull maker' and W. East who hired out boats. Lesser known names, F. Ruff boat-builder at Long Bridges and Folly Bridge made charges, as did J.H. Clasper, another boat-builder.[31] G.B. Hill appear to be the principal decorators to the barge, undertaking a refurbishment of 'painting and gilding the exterior to the barge', varnishing the inside and providing new blind with cords and tassels in 1876. An interesting appendage to this occurs in Sherwood's *Treasurer's Book* of June 1884, where he wrote that the barge needed decoration. Hill had given an earlier estimate of £150 – 'W.L. Courteney the current treasurer' decided to get a 'different style of ornamentation'; it would appear there was an element of friction in the final outcome. Plaisters of Oxford were providers of furnishings and rat traps, Badcocks upholsterers and cabinet makers, Elliston and Cavell the 'general outfitter' who supplied household goods and put down linoleum and floor cloth in the barge. Victualling was provided by Greenwood 'the Italian warehouseman', Park, the 'wine and spirit merchant', while Archers, Hawkins and Morgan kept the barge warm with coals for the hardy rowers. Cerebral interests were provided by Slatters, whose copious bills included supply of the *Field*, *Punch*, the *Sportsman*, *Oxford Chronicle*, *Telegraph*, *Graphic* and *The Times*, including 'refilling twelve blotters' on the barge. The barge appeared very much a home for the rowers, to relax, read, have tea, write letters, talk through the day's rowing and generally unwind.

Odd incidentals reoccur in the accounts. Mrs Grant made periodical claims for 'damage to meadow' at an almost annual cost of £3.00. Fosters, the tailors, supplied 'a drab double empire mackintosh', presumably for the boatman in 1877; Spiers for boat race charts; Burrow the saddler; Franklin for horse hire; and the indomitable-sounding Mrs Hicks hired

Charles Bossom's account to the OUBC October 1876

Foster's bill for Drab double Empire Mackintosh – 1877

By kind permission of the OUBC

out her pistols for the Fours and issued her bill of 1882 from the Salter's barge.

Trading terms were especially lenient, the norm seeming to be '5% charged if bill not settled at the expiration of six months' although boat builders' accounts once rendered seemed to be open to negotiation. Perhaps one of the strangest entries is recorded as 'experiements on barge at a cost of £6 3s 8d in June 1891' – it is to be hoped they were of a marine nature.

Sherwood's prized *'Treasurer's Private Book* 1878', a cream-bound ageing leather volume should be set in relation to these accounts as it contains 'his hints to future treasurers':

- keep out of debt (he was responsible for debts of £1032 in 1857 including the mortgage of the barge)
- Get your bills at the end of each term and pay them at once
- Get a written estimate before undertaking a work of considerable cost
- Do without a clerk; or if you have one let him have nothing to do with money matters. In 1854 the Club owed Grant, the clerk to the committee, £87 when building work began on the new barge – obviously this must have caused some friction. Sherwood, somewhat unchristianly for a man of the cloth, refers to Grant, after his death as 'a dictator' – apparently 'the committee could not always get their own way'.
- Beware of starting fresh gratuities (Tims had been given £20 in 1879 as a gift when he set up in business – Sherwood had questioned whether this payment was advisable – (pencilled note in the accounts).[32]

This is all probably sound advice, with the inference of a bruised bear. He recommended the following economies: doing away with a second waterman, the club should cease to stamp letters from the barge, the capitation fee (a type of membership levied to the rowers) should be increased and also mentioned the 'special train' from Moulsford as an unnecessary extravagance, believing that 'the ordinary trains are not unreasonably inconvenient'.[33] Innovatively he printed a set of accounts for each term showing income and expenditure, copies of which survive.

In 1881 the OUBC commissioned a purpose-built

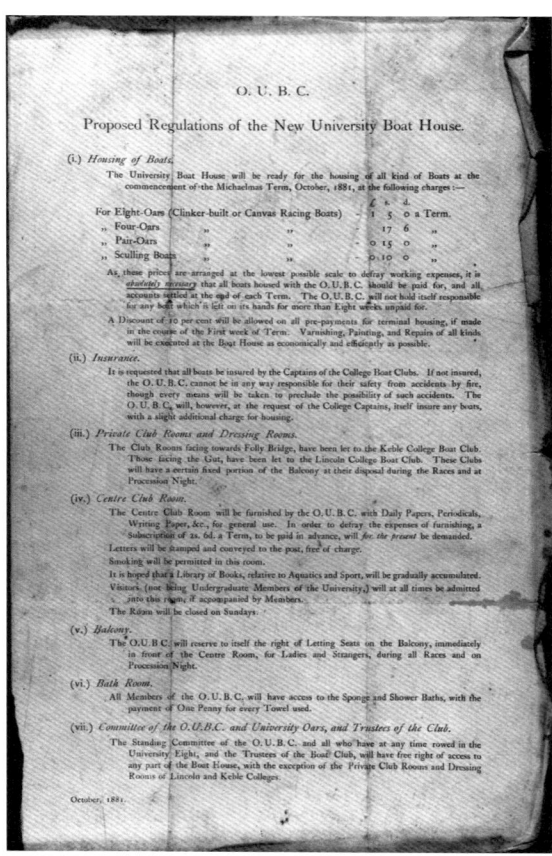

Oxford University Boat Club notice – April 1880
By kind permission of the OUBC

boathouse from John Oldrid Scott and this became a separate item in the accounts. Although the barge had been used as the clubhouse and office up to this date, (all correspondence notices and letters came from the barge), the brick-built building obviously now housed the greater part of the administration. A plot of land had been bought, according to Sherwood from 'Plowman' at a cost of £320 and the building of the boathouse was estimated at £485. Sherwood's account of the building, although not strictly pertinent to the history of the barges, is interesting as he discusses the choice of architect, musing over Jackson, Bodley (1827-1907), or Scott (probably John Oldrid) 'the first would perhaps do the most picturesque design'.[34] He also writes that the clubrooms facing Folly Bridge were let to Keble College Boat Club and that the rooms facing the Gut let to Lincoln, which is relevant information in terms of tracing the college barge occupation at that time.

The third set of accounts, an old red leather volume dated

OUBC Accounts Easter Term 1877
By kind permission of the OUBC

1894-1918, does not discriminate the separate headings of barge, boats, Boat Race or Henley. An entry for registration of the barge occurs, as do minor decorations, insurance and other subsistences previously listed. The expenditure notably lessens, bar the occasional charring bill. The more ominous 'blinds darkening order' of October 14th 1914 seems to close a chapter and bring a silent period to the barge. There are no entries for the barge during 1914-1918.

Norman Dix, the Univ waterman tells a sad story about the Varsity barge. Blackler, the waterman, *c.* 1940, lived on board and was known as a 'fair drinker', with regular habits at the pub. He returned to the barge one night on his punt and slipped over the side and was found drowned the next morning with a chain wrapped round his leg. Tims was so upset that he packed up his business and the barge changed hands, Norman believes about three times, until it was left for derelict and broken up by the Thames Conservancy at Osney. Landon Temple lived aboard the barge with his wife in the 1940s; they remember great parties, an ornate decorative programme and inordinately happy times. A rare interior shot of 1948 is provided by J. L.W. Bradbury.

These men, gathered from the Victorians, Edwardians and the changing twentieth century were the essential 'users' of the barges. They experienced life on these floating clubhouses from their own particular perspective, as rowers, boatmen, or houseboat owners. The next chapter steps back in time to describe the social life of the early Oxford oarsmen in the context of the University at that time.

Interior of the OUBC barge *c.* 1948
By kind permission of J.L.W. Bradbury

The University

MID-NINETEENTH TO MID-TWENTIETH-CENTURY BARGE USERS

Stone's edited version of the *University in Society* notes that Oxford, in the first half of the nineteenth century was a hotbed of 'aristocratic' values'; the students were mainly drawn from the upper echelons of society, the majority being public school educated.[35] The middle classes were in the main unable to afford the luxury of such education. The second quarter of the nineteenth century is highlighted as one of the most 'socially exclusive' in any period of the University's history. However Lawrence suggests the growth of the professional middle classes, with their new-found income from the 1860s onwards, enabled sons of merchants, land agents, bankers, schoolmasters, architects and civil servants to contribute to the dramatic rise of numbers at Oxford.[36] The Parliamentary Commission of 1852, which had reduced the cost of university education, inevitably opened the floodgates for a wider social integration.[37]

A new era of discipline was inaugurated to cope with these numbers; the students were apparently 'driven out of the pubs' and their energy diverted to rowing and cricket to coincide with the new moral ethic.[38] The 'games conscious' Victorians believed sport and physical prowess to be character forming and threw their spirits into competitive sport, centred on college identity. Discipline on the water was strict, fines were issued to those who failed to show up. The barges were ideal flagships to take this collegiate identity into the more public arena of the river, echoing as they did the architectural and sporting prestige of individual colleges.

Life was regimented for the nineteenth-century undergraduate, regulated by daily attendance at chapel and academic work. Green's *History of Oxford University* provides amusing anecdotal evidence of nineteenth-century rowing pranks: in 1880 a member of the University College Boat Club 'screwed up some of the dons' outer doors,' including the senior Proctor's (they were inevitably rusticated).[39] The majority of men up at Oxford were 'conventional' types, a mixture of normal undergraduate jokers, others of more aesthetic bent who 'committed the unpardonable offence of wearing ties of unusual tint' or 'used scent in chapel'.[40] Most however were conformist, with 'remarkably short hair', stiff collars and ties rigidly holding them together, heading for conventional careers in home office, politics, the church and law.[41] Women, admitted first to Lady Margaret Hall and Somerville in the late 1870s, were chaperoned and only eventually allowed to matriculate in 1920; they did not participate physically in the rowing but provided chorus support from the barges.[42] In the twenty-first century, this situation is now redressed, rowing being one of the most popular sports amongst women at Oxford.

The Oxford University Eight of 1908 shows contemporary rowing club dress, complete with individually-initialled sweaters and what appear to be alpaca or some type of furry trousers. The odd striped sock shows a hint of aestheticism with the ubiquitous canine mascot being *de rigueur* at the time. Green's account of a freshman, 'Elmhirst of Worcester … a conscientious but not an inspired student', taken from his diary 1911-12, reveals the life of a young man which revolved around the river, cricket, literary and college union.[43] An excerpt written at the end of Torpids, the winter rowing races, reads 'O.T. Jones had visitors about 12.15 last night, who awoke him by emptying two siphons of soda water in his bed and also smashed a picture and a walking stick'.[44]

When the First World War broke out Oxford 'emptied' and the examination schools were turned into a military hospital.[45] Green writes that even between the wars it was forbidden for an undergraduate to smoke in academic dress or to 'loiter at stage doors or attend a public race meeting' and that it was

The Oxford University Eight – 1908
By kind permission of the Master and Fellows of University College, Oxford

only after the Second World War that chapel became optional.[46] Harrison's *History of the University of Oxford* quotes Harold Macmillan describing Oxford after the war as 'a city of ghosts'.[47] Harrison describes how the falling middle-class birth rate meant that few families could now afford the average £250 expenses needed to support student life; those lucky enough to be there were 'in no hurry to grow up'.[48] Louis MacNeice writes somewhat arrogantly 'we products of the English public schools went to Oxford either for sport or beer drinking ... or for the aesthetic life and cocktails'; the public school ethos was still dominant in 'cultural, political, social and athletic' matters[49] Green writes that dons were a part of the student culture often taking long walks with their protegés 'attend[ing] undergraduate dinners and coaching rowing'. Dances in Oxford were still out of bounds and drinking only allowed in colleges, which often brewed their own beers. Those who escaped to London for other pursuits returned on a late train from Paddington known as the 'Fornicator'.[50] This however did not stop essential revelling. Inter-war Bumps suppers were renowned for their wild 'semi-tribal' behaviour, leaving, as Green writes, 'a trail of burnt furniture, shattered lavatory seats and elevated chamber pots'. It was he writes, 'overwhelmingly middle class', a student being a recognised type who wore grey flannels, tweed jackets, collar and tie or white flannels and blazer for sporting events.[51]

Harrison paints an amazingly privileged picture of undergraduate life at this time. Lunch and breakfast were usually served in their rooms, their beds made, coals brought up, clothes laid out and chamber pots emptied by the college servants, many of whom he writes, held longer tenure at the colleges than the fellows.[52]

By the 1920s class attitudes were changing: apparently half the undergraduates at Oxford received aid in one form or another. New social classes entered university life and inevitably change occurred. Green recounts Osbert Lancaster's description of the 'hearties' (credited as an Edwardian term) who were 'often elaborately plus-foured' or wore 'long striped scarves indicative of athletic prowess'.[53] Oxford bags were considered 'daring' and replaced the conformist flannels.

Green describes the immediate post-war intake as 'unusually mature'. By the 1950s and 1960s a new generation of undergraduates were clouded, with what Green describes, as a 'a mood of introspection'.[54] Public school boys did not now hold sway over the grammar school entrants and sex was no barrier; the 'independence of the undergraduate' crept in. Mike Day, undergraduate at St John's in the 1960s, son of an Oxford policeman, would probably endorse this; he writes, somewhat cautiously, of 'unofficial parties and romantic trysts' held on the St John's College barge.[55]

Life from the boatman's perspective may have been a little different. Norman Dix, the Univ waterman born in 1913, remembers the barges as a little boy of eight or nine years old, Norman's father being senior scout at University College, a great riverman, waterman and rower. George Bossom was the Univ waterman before Norman, a 'man of few words', and Ned Boles before that. Norman was simply referred to as 'boy'. His duties included at least one hour's manual pumping a day, stoking of the fire, cleaning and general maintenance. Norman had worked in college before the war, being in charge of the dining hall, so was well known to all the students. A great rower himself, Norman started the local club and became Honorary Secretary of the University College Servants Boat Club. Borrowing an eight and blades they won the Grand Challenge cup at the Oxford City Regatta in 1946.

Ned Bole's father was a great friend of the Talboys; he lived in a huge Victorian house near the side of Folly Bridge whose cellars were filled with boat cushions and poles. The other Talboys waterman was Dick who worked for the OUBC. Talboys owned a barge of their own and had a boatbuilding business in Thames Street with a big boathouse, building clinker fours and occasionally eights, all of which, Norman reminisces, is sadly 'swept away'.

Tims had a boatyard and boatshed with a huge woodshed which in the 1930s 'blew apart'.[56] R.T. Rivington writes that Tom Tims, son of John, who had worked at Salter's, lived on the Green Barge at Christ Church Meadow.[57] Halls had paddle steamers, Goatley was a boat builder and professional coach, the Beasleys were a waterside family, as were the Bossoms, one of whom was born on a barge. Clinkers were supplied by Salter's. Tims' boat business at Long Bridges was eventually bought by Walkers and Talboys. These river families provided the infrastructure necessary for the maintenance of rowing and the barges.

Clearly it is important in terms of collating the data on individual barges to establish the generic type and common characteristics. This is the purpose of the next chapter, which aims to look at the colleges who took inspiration from the OUBC, who were the 'front runners' in purchasing a livery barge. Later these colleges were responsible for commissioning the second generation, creating the first true Oxford College barges.

Norman and Boxer
Courtesy of Norman Dix

The Front Runners

THE COLLEGES WHO PURCHASED THE LIVERY BARGES:
THE ORIEL COLLEGE BARGES

A history of the livery company barges containing a chapter on the 'Oxford connection' was published by Dr Nicholls Palmer in 1997. The work concentrates on the livery barges and clearly explains the role of the colleges who purchased them.[58] This enquiry proceeds a step further in examining the archival evidence at each college in order to glean more insight into the college barges themselves.

In chronological terms it appears that Oriel College was the forerunner in purchasing what is believed to be the Goldsmiths' barge between the years 1848-50 (opinions vary as to precise date).[59] A fellow of Oriel, F. J. Varley, writes in a *Memorandum of the Oriel College Barge* that he believed the first Oriel barge was the Goldsmiths', who sold their barge *c.* 1850.[60] This date is corroborated by Timb's *Curiosities of London c.* 1867 which notes the livery company 'did not replace' the barge.[61] Richard Norton is confident that the Goldsmiths' barge, with its distinctive angels, did go to Oriel. Valuable archival evidence has now come to light which further substantiates this.

A letter in the Oriel archives from R.T.D. Sayle, the author of *The Barges of the Merchant Taylors' Company*, states his belief that Oriel owned the Merchant Taylors' barge, which they discarded in 1882-7; Norton is confident this is erroneous.[62] Salter's, the boat builders, stated that when they built the new (present day) Univ barge in 1878, they believed the old Merchant Taylors' barge had been broken up, which would negate Sayle's supposition. Varley notes that 'Oriel say they had the Merchant Taylors' barge up to about forty-five years ago and that the present one is a replica'; Norton similarly refutes this.[63]

The Oriel College Boat Club Accounts provide interesting documentary evidence to test such theories. The first dates from 1846. No mention is made of the barge; the first being rowing expenses in 1850 with a note 'a flag for the torpid'. Both boat-builders Hall and King were paid accounts in 1850, Hall's being a considerable £20 which could well have been the rental for a barge. 1858 marks the first mention of a barge in the Oriel accounts, which reads 'to Gill and Ward – repairing lock on the barge – 10s'. This obviously does not negate the theory of Oriel owning a barge prior to this date; casual book keeping was not unusual, however it is definitive proof of the existence of a barge from that date.

Entries for the barge increase after this and include such minutiae as stamps for the vessel. A larger expenditure of £16, which could have been maintenance or rental, marks the start of the barge accounts being separated from those of the Boat Club. A note dated January 1858 refers to 'a meeting was held in Mr Isaac's [King's] room – it was determined to raise the barge subscription from 10s to 16s'. Any student who used the barge or was a member of the Boat Club was obliged to pay an annual subscription; by this means the colleges raised funds to support their barges.

Interestingly, further entries reveal that a 'rent for barge' (£10) was paid to Goatley, a boatman, on a half-yearly basis from June 5th 1858 to November 14th 1859. Other entries include one for coals and three for brandy, a secondary warming agent seemingly necessary for the nineteenth-century rower.

In January 1860 and again in March of the same year Goatley was paid what appears to be a wage of £1.10s. An entry in the Summer Term 1860 makes note of £10 'for restoring the barge'. A new rental arrangement appears to have been made by November 13th of that year where Blake was paid for 'rent' to the barge. This is repeated through 1861 and 1862, after this date the accounts merge and disappear into a Boat Club record.

What is definitive from this evidence is that Oriel undoubtedly had a rented barge from 1858; it seems probable that someone, perhaps Goatley, actually owned the barge. Nicholls Palmer states that 'the [Goldsmiths] barge was reputedly sold to Oriel' in 1848 for £100.[64] To complicate matters further Sherwood mentions an Oriel College barge in 1857.[65]

The records are scant between these dates and similarly from 1862-92 when Oriel commissioned their new barge. Varley confirms: 'the Oriel barge lasted as an original down to 1892 and was rebuilt by Salter's to a design of

T. G. Jackson's Oriel College barge, 1892
By kind permission of the Provost and Fellows of Oriel College, Oxford and Gilman and Soame

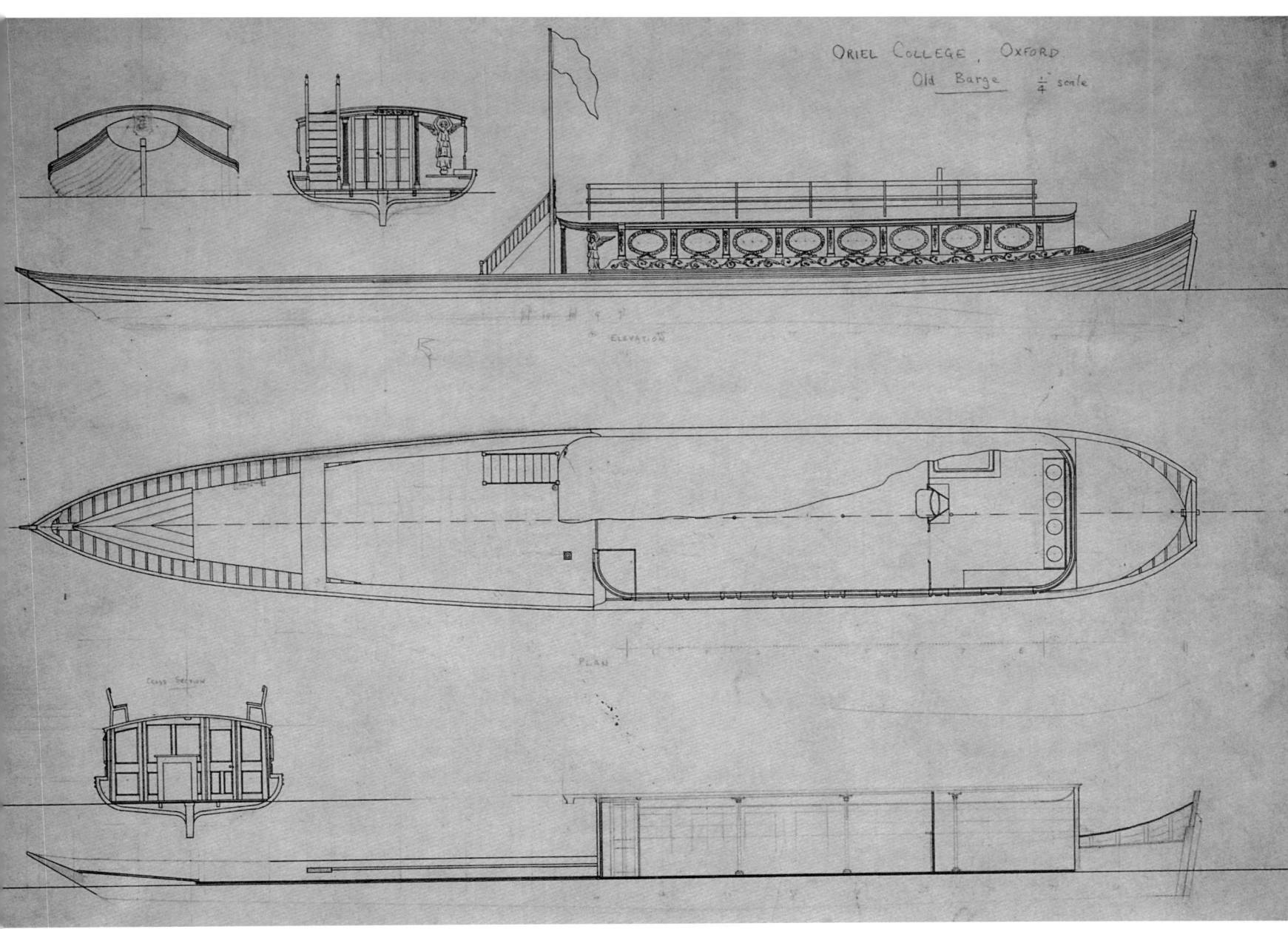

T.G. Jackson's pencil drawing of 'The Old Barge': plan, elevations and sections
Royal Academy of Arts, London

Sir Thomas Jackson'.[66] This was constructed 'following the lines of the old craft, and preserving its fitting and ornaments, including lead ornament and two gilded angels', the cost being £600 (information supplied by Canon Fellowes, according to Varley) 'being built by Salter's.' Varley adds that it 'was further embellished in 1921 as a memorial for the famous Oriel rowing blue, E.F. Henley'.

William Whyte of Wadham College, an expert on Jackson, throws further light on the subject. Jackson wrote in his *Recollections* of 1892 that this was 'my first attempt at boat building', being 'a copy of the city barge which the college had used until then.'[67]

The Captain's Record of 1892 records that 'a vote of thanks was given to the Treasurer for the great amount of trouble he had taken about the new barge which had arrived this term'; no further mentions of the barge seem to appear after this entry.[68]

The Royal Academy Archives hold T.G. Jackson's annotated design for the Oriel college barge; this consists of four pages of colour washed plans, sections and working diagrams.[69] They are a unique and exciting discovery in the history of the college barges, being the only full set of plans that have come to light so far. The fifth sheet contains a simple pencil drawing of 'Oriel College, Oxford – The Old Barge' (the Goldsmiths' barge) showing the distinctive angels, an elongated prow, the decorated foliate banding and eight oval windows rather than the ten of the 1892 barge. A stern-view sketch shows the stern complete with crest. The earlier barge layout had plain railings, much more deck space forward, making less 'house' and more barge.

The 'Design for Barge' No.1 is a particularly distinctive elevation, and appears to have been used for the 1892 barge. All four drawings are signed by T.G. Jackson and dated May 14th 1891; Salter Brothers (the builders) and William Henry Simmonds, possibly a clerk or legal representative, each put their signature to the sheets. The plan shows a 'Reading Room' being the main saloon, a closet under the stairs with urinal opposite, a boiler and stove amidships with the stove pipe standing 6'6" above the top deck. The dressing room and wash basins were situated to the rear of the vessel. Jackson notes that the 'stern [is] to be shaped like a boat and not like a punt'. Similarly the bow was to 'show like a boat-built barge and not like a punt'; his design intent to reproduce a barge proper is clear. The lower half of the railings were infilled with lattice work and the flag pole was to have pulleys.

The second sheet is of working drawings and confirms that 'this is one of the drawings referred to in the contract'. Jackson clearly stipulated 'the outside to be clinker built as showed and well nailed, caulked and made water tight'. It shows the construction of the hull to be predominantly of oak with elm. The railings were of wrought iron and 'screwed to [the] deck'. Also shown are the working plans of the fenestration with the details of the lead castings, painted in 'four oils' providing the detailed ornamentation of the barge. Mentioned are the '2 figures of victory next [to the] entrance, 2 bands of scroll work along gunwale, one on each side, 20 wreaths round windows, [and] 22 ornaments in panels of pilasters'. The latter showed a lion's head with ring, below which was a foliate drop; the other features an umbrella-shaped classical ornament capped by the head of an axe.

The third and fourth sheet provide further working details, a section of the staircase, hull and the partition between the reading and dressing rooms and details of the fireplace, with 'York slips'. The set of drawings are unique in the history of the barges, particularly as Salter Brothers, who built the majority of the barges, lost all their documents in a fire at their Oxford premises.

The twentieth-century *Captain's Records* make some

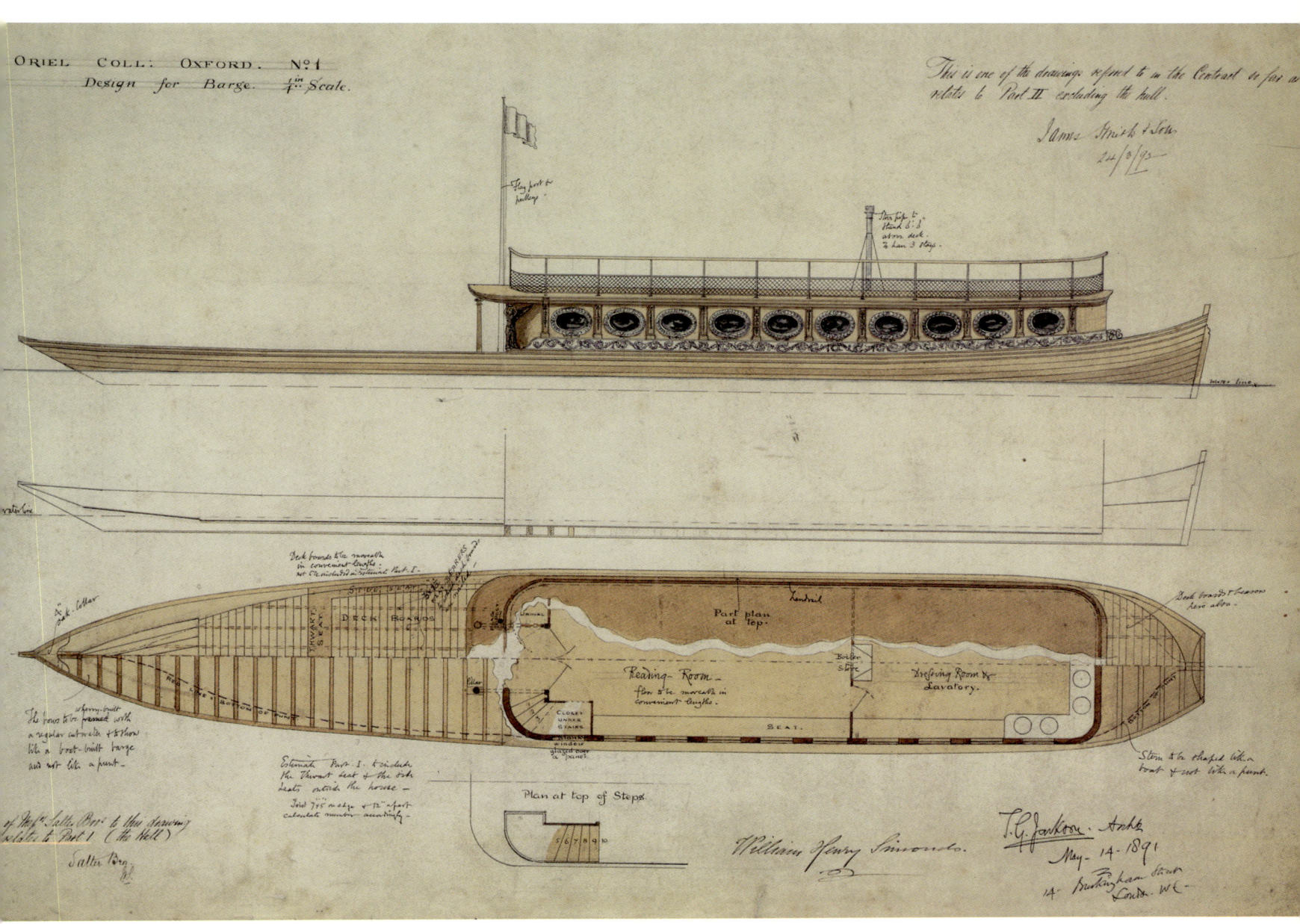

T.G. Jackson's design for the Oriel barge: plan and elevation of hull and superstructure
Royal Academy of Arts, London

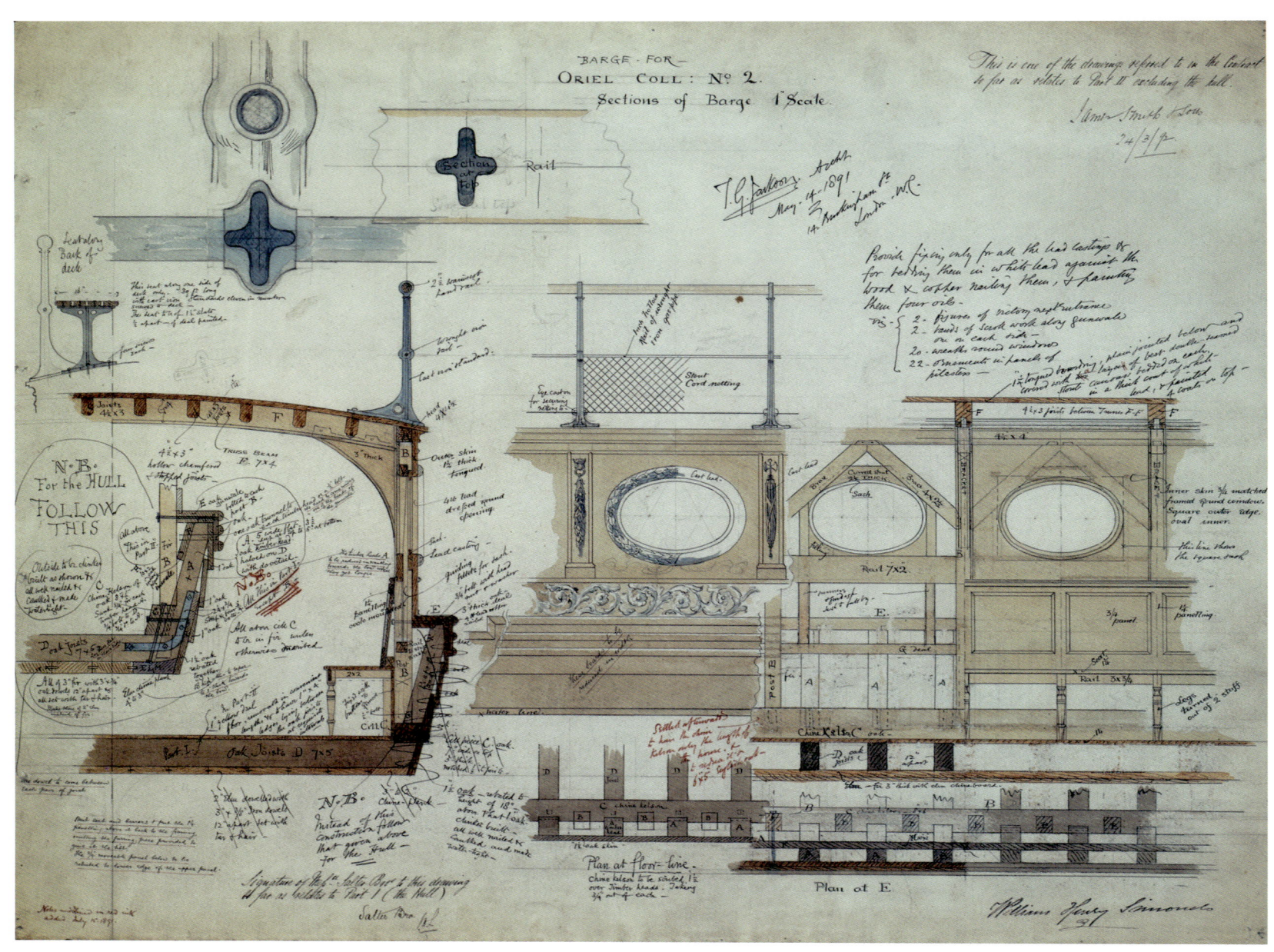

T.G. Jackson's contract drawings of the Oriel barge: sections of barge
Royal Academy of Arts, London

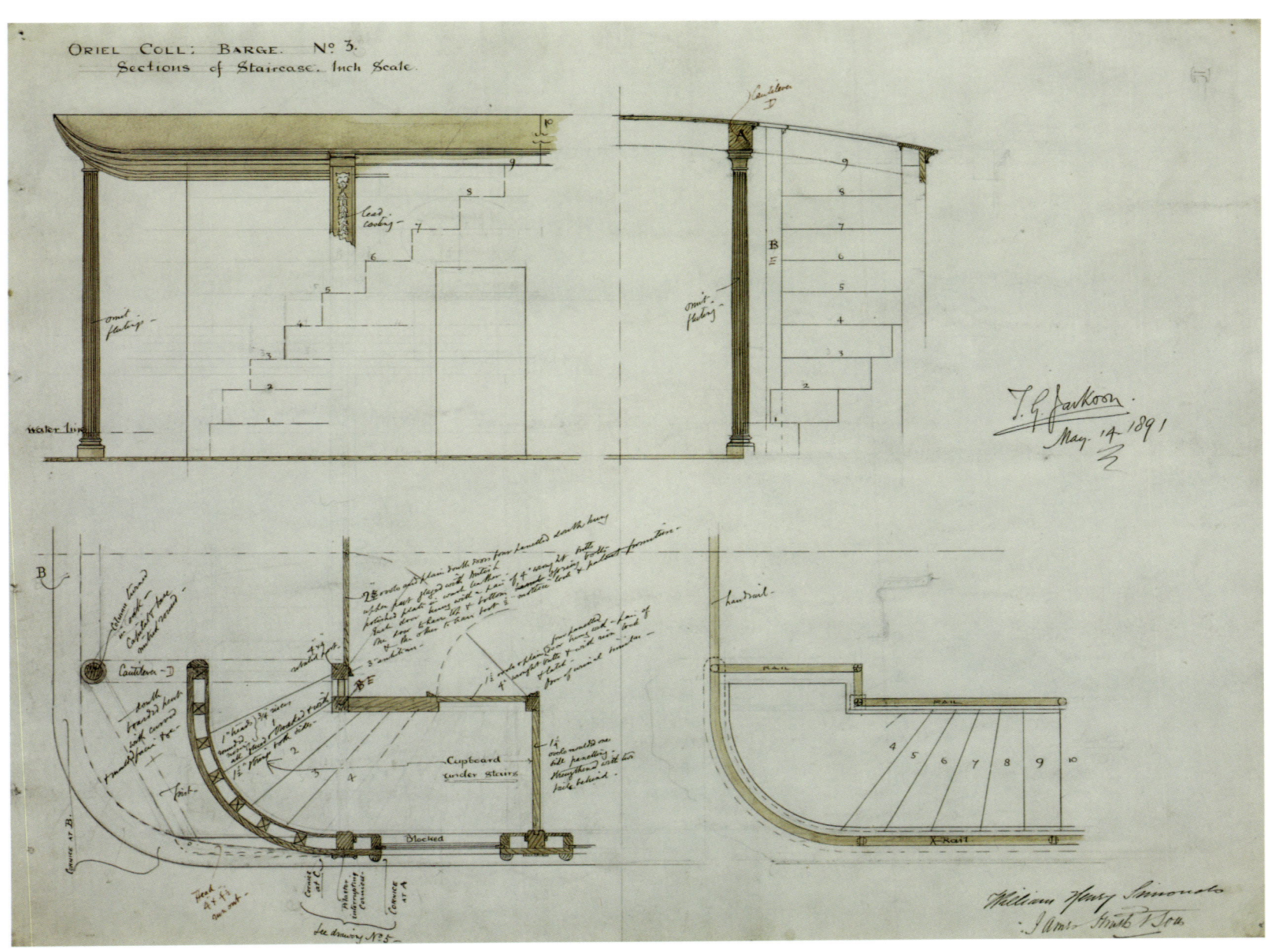

T.G. Jackson's contract drawings of the Oriel barge: sections of staircase
Royal Academy of Arts, London

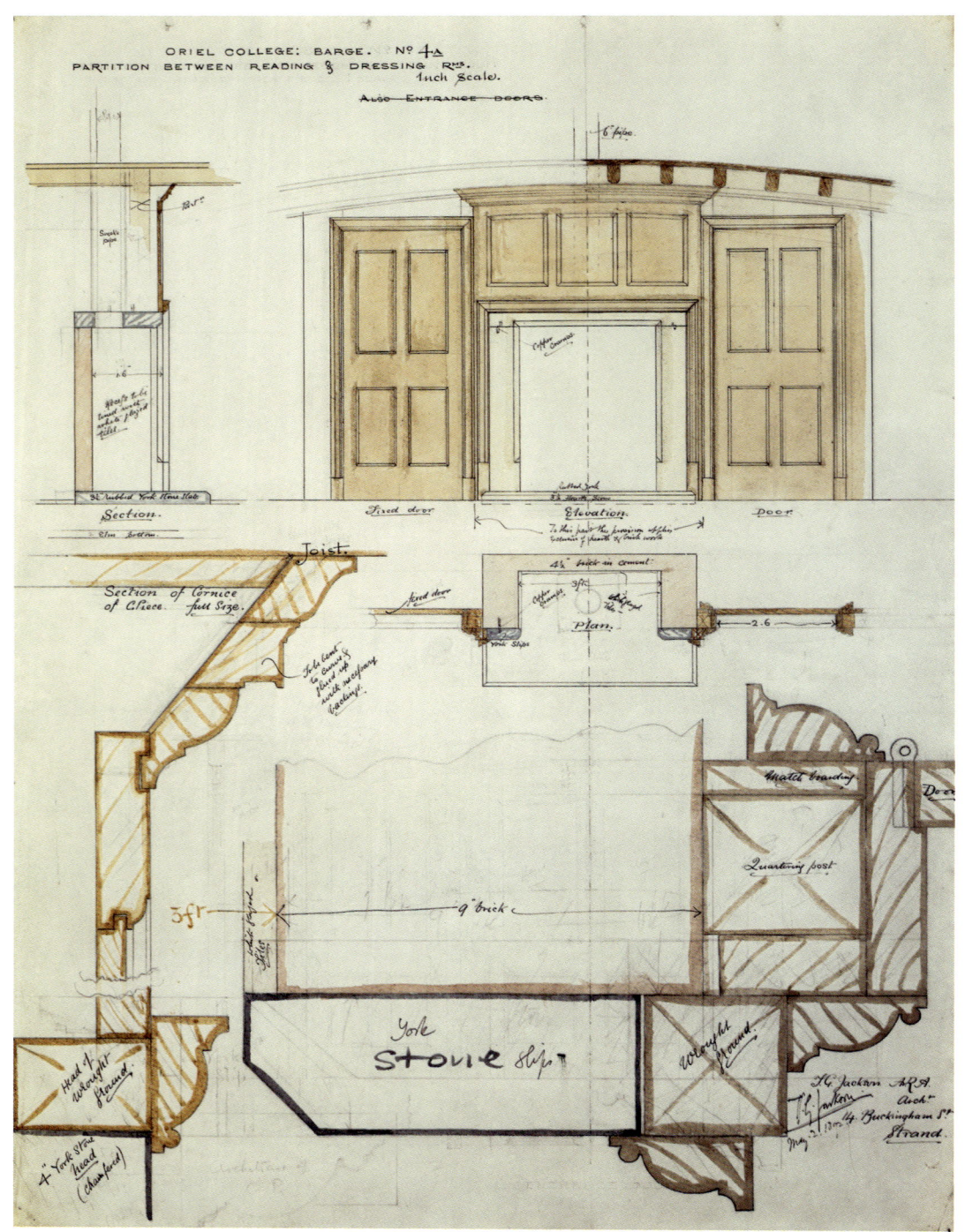

anecdotal reference to the barge: 'being bumped opposite it' and 'freshers attend[ing] daily at the barge for tubbing'.[70] An interesting reference in 1926-7 notes that 'various people threatened to strike, the General Strike of this year must have left an impression, but chiefly owing to the Dean they were persuaded to row'. No doubt a bit of extended energy and pain was thought to put paid to such misguided ideas. During 1939-40 boat club activity was stalled owing to the onset of war. Oriel shared their barge 'and resources with Hertford Boat Club'[71]. Dr E. Boardman, Oriel's archivist did locate an agreement dated 24th May 1943 'for tenancy of the barge as a Fire Boat Station until the end of the war'; an example of the barge's versatility. Norman Dix, the Univ waterman, kept the Oriel barge from the late 1940s in 'pump service using a portable pump every day until her demise'. The barge is believed to have been broken up in 1954 at Salter's slipway; two of her distinctive angels still decorate the purpose-built Oriel boathouse.

Opposite: T. G. Jackson's contract drawings for the Oriel barge: elevation and details of partition between reading and dressing rooms
Royal Academy of Arts, London
Right: one of the Oriel Victory Angels

THE UNIVERSITY COLLEGE BARGES

University College joined Oriel in the roll call of primary initiators of the Oxford barge tradition by purchasing the Merchant Taylors' barge from the OUBC in 1854.[72] The OUBC *Captain's Book* 1855-70 has an entry dated 1865 which states that 'Merton bumped New College opposite the Univ College Barge'.[73] A photograph is extant in the University College archives (see page ten) showing the Eight of 1862 on board the old Merchant Taylors' barge.[74]

Little written evidence is available in the college records. A note, which shall remain anonymous, in the Univ College Boat Club's second volume of 1892-1909 suggests that 'G.G. Bradley, Dean of Westminster, is the man to whom it is due that all our records have been cut – may he roast in hell'.[75] The pursuit of rowing versus a life of academia was a contentious issue, much as it is today.

A few good anecdotal references can be gleaned from the notebooks kept by the Captain of Boats: on April 19th 1872

The Univ barge 1907
By kind permission of the Master and Fellows of University College, Oxford

'Buffy was undressed in the Barge, his breeches hoisted half-mast height. He found the *Daily News* a most convenient garment and is going to row in this costume in the races'. Bumps that year cannot have been good, the entry 'worse and worse – Univ becoming weak and go like a hearse' is pretty soulful criticism. It is belived Univ took 'the Red barge', the Stationers' city barge in 1873.[76] A good photograph exists in the 1866 Album.

In October 16th 1876 a rather desperate entry reads: 'Barge sinking fast' indicating further depressing problems were hitting the Boat Club. Much pumping was done and wages had to be raised in consequence. A further caustic comment, dated October 18th 1876, notes a new cloth was purchased for the top of the barge 'in anticipation of its coming wreck'. The barge was eventually broken up at Osney in the summer of 1903.

In 1878 University College had the foresight to commission John Oldrid Scott, second son of George Gilbert

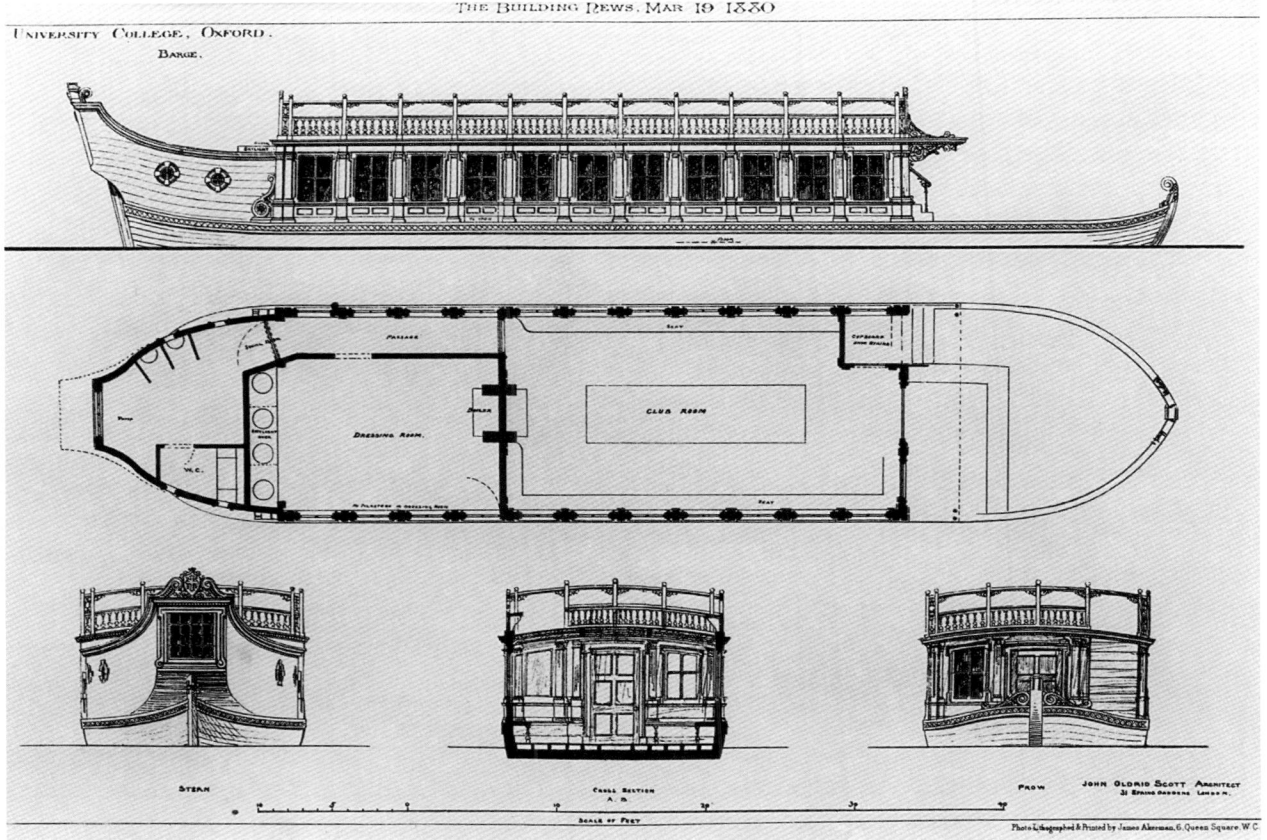

John Oldrid Scott's designs for the University College barge of 1878
The Building News – 1880

Scott (1811-78) who designed the Albert Memorial in Hyde Park, to draw up designs for the second University College barge. The college therefore joined Oriel and Corpus Christi in using prominent architects of their day. Scott's designs were published in the *Building News* of 19th March 1880, showing an elegant barge of simple classical decoration, having twelve rectangular sash windows intersected by pilasters. A swooping stern revealed a pair of oeil de boeuf windows to either side and a double casement, above which sat the college arms. Two decorated consoles appear to support the overhang of the upper deck, the flagpole rising from the decks below. The balustrading was decorated with ball finials, having a gentle curve to bow and stern.

An entry in the *Captain's Book* dated February 22nd 1888 notes 'the barge was rightly, I think, crowded with rank, fashion and beauty, most conspicuous being Mr Dendy and Mr Chavasse'. The Univ archives are particularly rich in their photographic collection, which includes examples of contemporary rowing dress.

The 1878 barge was built at Streatley by Samuel Saunders in 1878 and 'fitted up' at Caversham; a pencilled rough wooden plaque found in the restoration of the Univ barge confirms this. It could well be that the East Boat Building Company of Caversham, whose name appears in the New College barge files, was the company who executed this work.

No further documentary evidence exists from that period, save one letter discovered by the Univ archivist, Dr Darwall-Smith from F.W. Hall dated 12th May 1921 which throws light on second generation 'college barge' design and the college's historical sensitivity. Hall wrote

> The barge is no doubt longer than most (tho' it overlaps Queens to a certain extent) because for sentimental reasons we determined to build it in the same style as the one which it displaced – i..e. on the lines of the old city barges with a rowing space in the bows. But the barge proper is probably smaller than most.

In 1922 extensive repairs were undertaken by Salter's to the hull and flooring of the barge costing £800. Fire on the college barge was inevitably a dramatic incident. *The Record* of 1932-1933 writes that the interior was virtually destroyed when fire broke out.[77] The Chief Fire Officer Eldridge with seven officers and men participated in a 'thrilling dash' across the meadows to save the barge. Norman Dix, Univ boatman

The Univ barge – fitted up at Caversham 1878
By kind permission of David Sherriff

The Univ barge photographed with the VIII in 1864. This is the Red (Stationers') barge
By kind permission of the Master and Fellows of University College, Oxford

from 1946, recalls that most of the brigade were well known to the watermen on the river; pumping out a sinking barge was well within their remit. The fire was apparently 'fiercest round the fireplace' and may have been started from drying clothes on an easel by the fire, or simply just by 'dry panelling catching alight'. Someone in the know attached a note stating the former 'to the mast with a kitchen utensil'. Luckily the windows had been closed by George Bossom, the waterman, at 6.30 p.m.

The event was recorded in the *Oxford Mail* of 16th February 1932, but perhaps gets greater coverage in the *University Boat Club* Volume IV.[78] This recounts that Dick Talboys saw the fire at 7.30 pm coming from the bottom of the chimney and immediately telephoned the college; various undergraduates including 'Gridland Holland and Tomkin' sprinted down. The changing room was billowing with smoke and buckets were employed until the fire brigade, somewhat delayed by the opening of the meadow gates, got to the scene. Water damage is particularly destructive; pictures, books and valuables had been rescued; the barge sank in mud to her stern. It was discovered later that the barge was not insured, but the College insurance company gallantly came to the rescue. After the fire in April it was decided 'to put the old tub in a thoroughly good state of repair'. The hull was re-tarred, upper deck re-canvased, hot water put into the changing rooms alongside the cold shower, new hemp matting in the saloon and changing room and, most importantly, a new chimney was installed. A 'committee of taste' was set up who chose new covers for armchairs, new curtains 'with gold braid and a new tablecloth'. The Univ rose again.

The interior is rather evocatively portrayed in the *College Record* of 1967: 'inside leather, varnished panelling, ageing sepia photographs, litter of oars and rudders, … the vivid colours of Fuller fancy cakes, Dundee cakes, Leander ties, shrunken caps, old Bossom and Norman Dix, (known as 'Boy' to Bossom), alert and smiling at his elbow'.[79] Norman refutes this, saying Bossom 'never' smiled at him.

Norman Dix still has that twinkle in his eye and is a fount of knowledge on the barges, with a redoubtable memory of his lifetime spent on the river as waterman to University College. When Bossom retired in the 1950s, with 'two bad knees', Norman took on full responsibility for the barge, ferry punt, and boating of the Univ men. The barge needed pumping twice a day; this was done manually and took at least an hour of heavy work. Norman remembers the barge being taken up to Salter's for repairs in the 1950s; she was pulled up on a slipway and was so rotten her stern 'dropped off'; it was possible to push a finger through it with a gap through to the dressing room. In restoration they found that the floor was built as part of the hull in an immovable solid piece. Eventually this was reconstructed in six separate sections with the work being almost complete for the summer race week. A stipulation was laid down by Salter's, however, that no more than fifty should be on the upper deck at any one time.

Norman remembers being down river helping with the start of racing; he received an urgent message to return to the barge which was listing dramatically. To his horror her upper deck was laden with over two hundred students, Master and all. The order to 'abandon ship' was quickly carried out; the Master, Professor A.L. Goodhart, (1951-1963) had difficulty understanding why the Univ was not as robust as she should have been, having just spent £1500 on her restoration. Norman recalls him saying 'Am I the first Master to be evicted from the Barge?' Water had entered the aft end, the fire brigade were employed yet again, the 'dear undergraduates' helped and the barge, pumped out, lived to see another day. Apparently Goodhart never set foot on the barge again.

Norman recalls hilarious and very happy days with the Univ, such as rag racing when every conceivable club participated in college run 'tub fours' with comic results. 'The victor was to buy half pints for all and consume on the spot'.

The College Record of September 1967 noted that 'to the regret of all save the modernists the college barge was sold for £300 in September 1965'.[80] The prospect of further extensive repairs, alongside the newly reverted OUBC lease had negated the use of the barge. Professor John Albery FRS, legendary Master of Univ (1989-1997) was a fabulously keen supporter of the Univ in exile, but voted most definitely for her extraction from the college accounts. The college shield was taken down and an anonymous eulogy, dated 10th May 1976, along with a pencil sketch of the barge sums up the sadness:[81]

> And so she had to go
> Was sadly moved away
> Instead the water flow
> The gap remains today
>
> Toll for the Barge!
> Stout Bossom has now gone
> His last load poled across
> His ferrying done
>
> The dripping landing stage
> Where Univ boats made fast:
> the roof where every age
> Has watched Eights racing past.
>
> The cheerful cabin's glow
> The pictures on each wall
> The oars of famous crews
> Sweet cakes and teas for all
>
> A floating common room
> Set in a silver stream
> This seat of Isis, whom
> all hold in high esteem.
>
> All this is now a dream
> Our Barge's days are o'er
> Proud prow and painted beam
> Shall ride the Thames no more

The barge was sold to a local boat builder and used as a boat repair shed for Hubbards who serviced punts above Folly Bridge.

However all was not lost. John Wolstenholme, an old member and keen supporter of the Boat Club rallied his fellow members in a brave effort to purchase the barge, which came up for auction in July 1987. Other forces were afoot. They were outbid by an antiques dealer from Marlborough, an unfrocked Catholic priest. Biding his time at the auction was another player, David Sherriff, a Thames marina owner with a penchant for the old, the quirky and the beautiful in maritime history. Being a mite canny and with the disposition of a bull terrier he did not bid at the auction, but approached the purchaser afterwards and lured him back to his Wiltshire home, extraordinarily three miles from Marlborough. He plied the hapless dealer with good claret and explained to him that he had bought a white elephant and that the rightful and logical owner was himself, David Sherriff. Cheques passed hands wildly in the night and the rest is Sherriff's history.

Wolstenholme became a supporter of Sherriff and established himself as go-between par excellence in introducing the old members to the new owner. He writes 'Sherriff masterminded what must be a unique restoration' – it is believed to be the only existing Oxford college barge with fully-renewed timber hull, including the greater part of the superstructure, which with luck and maintenance should survive a further hundred years.

The barge was brought back to Thames and Kennet Marina, at Caversham, where, by some odd coincidence she was fitted up in 1878. People laughed on its journey from Oxford and many doubted the possibility of restoring this decrepit mustard-coloured 78' barge. Water poured from her sides when nails were pulled out and the superstructure looked near to crumbling. She was valiantly lifted by the Terranova crane company in canvas slings and filmed by Southern Television for a news bulletin on the 25th June 1988. During lifting one of the spreader beams protecting the superstructure broke; the barge dropped visibly by feet, the sides crumbled but miraculously she came to rest on blocks, nearly in one piece. The restoration programme was on. A Wiltshire carpenter, James Clements was put to work full time with an impossible schedule of six months set to rebuild her. Boat building experience was brought up from Cowes, and Sherriff, whose lifetime has been devoted to boats (he built the police boats on the Thames and Londinium 11 for the Port of London Health Authority in 1976) with meticulous care ordered twenty tons of thirty-year-old seasoned English oak, 40,000 nails, 108 phospher bronze keel bolts, 20,000 brass screws and one mile of teak decking during the period 20th December 1987 to 25th June 1988. A courteous and dry-humoured Welshman, Lewes Carroll, from Wiltshire, was in charge of painting along with James Clements, an experienced house carpenter; they jointly constituted the main task force under the ever-hovering presence of Sherriff. The hull was fully rebuilt, twenty-four new sash windows replaced, replica panelling and pilasters inserted, tanks fitted, a galley constructed, carpet woven in Univ colours and twenty-four sets of curtains made by the writer of this history. Wolstenholme was suitably impressed by the 'super loos'. The old gutters were eliminated and a new staircase installed. The old barge clock that Ronnie Rowe broke in 1936, when taking down a blade, was put back and still stands at 17.49, particularly appropriate as University College celebrated its 750th anniversary in 1999.

A Univ cap worn by C.W. Key in 1888 and two blades along with the college arms were proudly presented to the care of David Sherriff for the Univ barge. Additionally Pamela Wolstenholme donated a copy of *The Rower*, a painting which had reputedly hung on the barge in the 1930s. She is a scantily-dressed young woman, clad in knickers, not normally worn by her sex at that time. The painting executed by Lancelot Glasson (1894-1950), 'a talented amateur of Cumberland,' was supposedly the subject of some discussion; legend goes that the person in question was 'reputed to have changed on the barge'. The original hangs in Rochdale Art Gallery who have investigated the provenance of the painting. Suggestions have been made that in fact *The Rower* was painted by Dame Laura Knight, known to have a sense of humour, who entered it for the Royal Academy Summer Exhibition of 1932 under a pseudonym as a joke, for which it was nominated 'Picture of the Year'.[82]

Wolstensholme's article in the *College Record* also recounts the story of the Univ ghost, a 'red haired man, with mouth turned down at the left corner'. A medium was later to confirm his existence on board. Clements and Carroll, the newly-designated house boat restorers, both complained of the Univ's frame shaking uncontrollably whilst on blocks and under canvas for the long winter of 1988. At times they were visibly frightened; they had no previous knowledge of the ghost. Similarly I can recount a story of one winter's afternoon when I entered the barge to retrieve two tables at the far end of the saloon. Knowing the light switches to be further into the bowels of the barge, (and being somewhat fearful) I did this mid-afternoon with the intention of returning to collect the tables, placed near the main door, at the end of the day. When I returned at five o'clock the tables were back at the far end of the saloon.

Sherriff, with some sponsorship from Courage Breweries, finally took the Univ to the Henley Regatta of 1987. The Univ was placed virtually on the starting line by the cautious committee of the Henley Regatta, uncertain of this new phenomenon attending their prestigious event. Jazz bands, champagne and arrival by helicopter were all part of the experience in those exuberant days and Henley, with apprehension, showed guarded support. As the years went on, with good behaviour, the Univ has progressed up the Regatta course, and now holds the best position for a craft of her size on the Bucks station, in full, and we suspect rather enviable view from the grandstand. So much so that we were told if you tuned into the Henley Regatta on their website at one time, the image that appeared was the Univ barge. University College are undoubtedly still proud of their barge; their present Master, Lord Butler, has continued the tradition of a 'Univ' day at Henley every year.

Forty old members formed the Univ Barge Society and met for the first time at Henley since before the First World War, attending the 150th Regatta on 28th June 1989. It is undoubtedly due to the trio of Professor John Albery, John Wolstenholme and David Sheriff, that the Univ has given such inordinate pleasure, retained its college connections and raised substantial sums for rowing and charities in its post-Oxford days.

After her restoration the Univ was renamed by George Harrison's wife, Olivia and has been used for all sorts of parties including undergraduates, politicians, pop stars, computer companies and splendid private parties hosted by John Albery and David Sherriff. She has lived her new life to the full, during sporadic periods at Henley, a trip up river to Chelsea Harbour in London, Bumps Weeks and a visit to Oxford in 1999 to celebrate Univ's 750th anniversary.

A few years ago a mysterious phone call came through from a ship's captain, enquiring whether it would be possible to view the Univ, late one winter's afternoon. The captain

The Young Rower – Lancelot Glasson 1932 *By kind permission of Rochdale Art Gallery, the Bridgeman Art Library and the Glasson Family*

represented someone of significance, but would say no more than that. As dusk approached the entourage arrived. Both Maurizio Gucci and his companion were totally enchanted with the barge. They had plans to take her as a private dining club, possibly on a Swiss lake. Gucci's Captain said he would be in touch. Calls were put through the following week expressing a definite interest and negotiations started, only to be broken off a few days later by his murder.

For the greater part of the year, however, the Univ rests and hibernates at Caversham; sometimes rumination starts as to her future. Her role as party palace and fund-raiser is a continuing tribute to the players involved.

The Univ barge 1980s
By kind permission of David Sherriff

The Exeter College Barges

Exeter College joined the roll call of primary initiators by purchasing the Stationers' Company barge in 1856, built by Searle in 1826. Richard Norton is 'certain that Exeter were using the Stationers' barge by 1850' and is also 'pretty confident that Exeter never actually owned her'.[83] The barge eventually became known as the 'Red Barge'. Norton describes the window surrounds as being red, with two red bands decorating the edge of the upper deck.

Sherwood writes that Exeter 'hired from Hall', the boatman, in the early years. Exeter's librarian, Mrs Topliffe, writes that in the nineteenth century the college also had a barge from Isaac King's yard; this was known as the Green Barge, which was used by the Barge Club.[84] Richard Norton's appendix to Nicholls Palmer's book confirms that Exeter had two barges from 1860-1872; presumably his source is Sherwood. A further reference in the OUBC *Captain's Books* at the Bodleian records that 'Oriel bumped Wadham at the Exeter barge on May 21st 1857'; this refers to the old Stationers' barge. An early photograph of 1873 shows this resplendent vessel with great swooping stern; there is a similar one of 1869.

The Stationers' barge photographed in 1873
By kind permission of the Master and Fellows of University College, Oxford

The second Exeter barge was built by Salter's in 1873 and was the subject of heated wrangling. The college Boat Club ledgers hold a 'A Full Account', dated Easter 1877, of the proceedings for construction of the new barge. This barge was 'placed on the river in 1873', but Salter's, as was often the custom, submitted their bill three years later in 1876, 'in excess of what had been expected.' The 'Full Account' looks to future boat clubs not to fall prey to such tactics. The raising of funds for the barge only realised a paltry £13 17s at first attempt. The money was returned to the members with a letter of thanks and the subsequent battle with Salter's for 'the barge bill' took on new proportions. One particularly contentious item was 'compensation for site' billed at £100, meaning hire of site. Salter claimed this to be 'a recognised charge on every barge on the river'. There was apparently a parallel with the Christ Church barge, where

The New Exeter barge in 1874
By kind permission of the Rector and Fellows of Exeter College, Oxford.

£40 was paid in similar circumstances. Exeter, unable to agree with Salter, consulted solicitors. Salter claimed he had paid £100 to Hall for the position of the Red Barge (this was refuted by the late Mr Hall's son who could find no record of the transaction in the accounts). Such disagreements were not uncommon between boat-builders and their clients. The outcome, recounted by R.B. Preston, the Hon. Secretary of 1877, dated Easter of that year, 'was to be that the Sub Rector, in conjunction with a certain friend of his was willing to lend such a sum to the Boat Club, magnanimously with interest.' The barge was mortgaged to him and the first repayment of £50 made at the end of 1877. An extra 10 shillings was levied on the Boat Club subscription and Salter's bill of £469 was eventually 'agreed' at £375 – the moral of the tale being to make sure bills are submitted on receipt of goods.

An article in the *Stapeldon Magazine* of 1953 notes that the barge, 'the oldest on the river' (eighty years at the time of writing) was taken out of the water and refitted by Salter's, relationships obviously having improved by then. The top deck joists were noted as 'safe' and there was talk of fitting a copper hull at £1,500. The piece continues that 'it is evident that the barge is doomed' and subsequently denigrates the modern purpose-built 'Boat House Alley'. The lament continues 'no more the staff making tea, the oars in their racks, the indomitable George (the Exeter boatman) not to speak of the records and photographs of past crews'.

A rather good epitaph remains to the Exeter college barge, unrecorded in its archives, and contributed by an anonymous donor. It apparently 'disappeared naturally', being pulled out on the 'green bankside of the Cherwell'. A waterman, 'friend and rascal,' found valuable recycling material up the Cherwell. The Exeter barge had a double skin of timber that was put to good use.

THE BALLIOL COLLEGE BARGES

Chronologically, Balliol was the next college to take up the livery barge call by purchasing the Skinners' Company barge in 1859.[85] The Balliol Boat Club Accounts start in the year 1835; the first entry in that year is 'Jack for house boat – £6'. The first mention of a barge proper comes with an entry dated April 27th 1837 'bought two pieces of crockeryware for the barge'. A later entry dated November 16th 1838 shows a debit of £45, a considerable sum, paid to Isaac King; this could well have been one year's rental or even a payment for the purchase of a barge. A further 'bounty to boatbuilder' of £1 was also paid. *The Balliol Boat Club Journal* of June 1838 records an entry for 'a dozen towels marked Balliol Barge'. June 11th of the following year indicates that Jack was paid two payments totalling £7 for the barge, which included a broken window; seemingly vandalism is not peculiar just to twentieth-century Oxford. Jack was similarly remunerated in 1841; these payments were most probably his boatman's wages. There are three interesting every day entries for 1839: a 5d debit for 'lad fetching jackets', the notable sum of £1 for a 'dog towel' and a further 7s 3d, part of which involved the payment for more broken windows.[86] In 1842 the barge was painted and furniture purchased for it. An entry of 1843, dated May 11th, notes to 'hire of the barge £5.00' and thereafter there are six entries up to 1846 and others up to 1848 for either hire of the barge, or attributed to Heather. By 1850 King was paid £19.15s for barge hire, which would suggest a different barge was employed or King had bought Heather's barge.

The Account Ledgers 1851-75 continue the story. King was paid for rental from 1851 to 1858. Entries occur for Combs, who may have been a boatman, 'a nipper for jackets' and George West 'for use of a barge at Henley' in June 1855. The tradition of colleges taking their barges to the Regatta was established by this time.

In 1857 a note to all secretaries was posted in the account book recommending they pay King one term in arrears to prevent 'confusion in the accounts and overcharging on his part'. Perhaps they had been in correspondence with Exeter College. In October 1858 King gave up his business; this is recorded in the Balliol Boat Club account. The college debt to him at this time was roughly £164; this was cleared by May 1859. The Balliol Boat Club journal confirms that in the Lent Term of 1859 the barge was 'purchased from the Skinners' Company for use of the college'.

Various entries from two brushes for the barge, soap, printing admission cards, water for the barge, painting, fires and club subscription to the OUBC all convey the general needs of its users and their requirements at the time. The year 1863 witnessed a royal visit to Oxford by the Prince and Princess of Wales, the cost borne on the Balliol College barge amounted to nearly £3.[87] In 1866 the barge is first referred to as the 'Balliol Barge' in the accounts, although there is probably little significance in this.

The accounts proceed through the 1870s in regular manner until 1879 when there is a note 'that the charge for rent and attendance (on the barge) was reduced from £38 10s to £35'. In October 1880 Salter's' outstanding debt of £150 was paid off. In 1881 2s 6d was charged for 'pumping of the barge during the Procession of Boats' – an ominous sign. An entry of 1881 notes a payment of £100, after this *The Boat Club Account* of 1869-94 recounts that 'the old Barge was rented for about 3 years'. Norton writes that the Skinners' barge was bought by Queens' in 1885; there does not appear to be any definitive date from the Balliol college records.[88]

From December 1880 'the question of a new barge' was in the hands of a sub-committee of Balliol men. This was realised as in the October Term 1881, A.L.Smith wrote: 'the barge which, from its plans, promises to be one of the finest on the river'. A vote of thanks was proposed to Dr Darbishire 'for the services he rendered the college in connection with this new barge'.[89] This appears to be the only entry in the Boat Club records concerning the new barge; there are no plans or architect's drawings.

Accounting entries of 1882-3 included the entries for coals, lifebuoys in 1889, magazines and stationery from Slatter and Rose including periodicals such as *Punch*, which seemed to be a basic prerequisite of nineteenth-century barge life. Repairing the barge clock, a new chimney in 1893, 'binding books for the barge', various barge movements, Procession Night expenses, fire insurances, new mooring bridge, repairs and poles, and Mrs Hicks's endless supply of pistols were all recurring expenses. On September 30th 1884 a bill for 'seven nights attendance on the barge' was obviously deemed necessary as a precaution against vandalism or pranks of some nature. Salter's bills appear to have been paid from 1886 through to the 1890s. R.B. Turton at this time provided a loan for the barge and was repaid in instalments of £50.

Balliol's Boat Club accounts stand out as exemplary barge evidence. Being meticulously kept, they probably excel any others, bar those of the OUBC. They appear to have been supremely organised too in issuing a separate set of Henley accounts. In 1892 an advertisement was sent out to magazines and newspapers, the *Field*, *The Times*, *Standard*, *Daily News*, *The Statesman* and *Oxford Magazine*, notices were also put up in London clubs, Atheneum, Brooks's, The Carlton, Reform, Ipthmion and rather exotic sounding Cocoa Tree, inviting application for Henley tickets. It appears Balliol took their barge to Henley from this time, during the first decade of the next century up to 1914. Entries include the cost of luncheons, decorating the barge with flowers, hire of tents, washing of linen, beds, ferrying, telegrams and hire of ground behind the barge in 1899, to the cost of £2 10s from the

Henley Regatta Committee. Quite considerable sums were spent on strawberries, cream, flowers and lobsters (the latter alone cost £7 in 1911).

Turn-of-the-century accounts reveal bills in 1904 for a 'canvas cover for the barge', recovering barge furniture in 1906, dredging under it in 1909 and a new flag and curtains in 1912, interspersed amongst general maintenance work.

In 1913 the Balliol Boat Club was given an endowment of £500 by Mrs K.J. Backhouse in memory of her husband who died in 1912 aged 26.[90] *The Balliol Record* of those fallen in the Great War makes sad reading. A second Barge Fund was set up in 1925, the timbers were deemed so rotten it was not thought wise to use it during Eights Week. Kindly and comforting comments flowed in from old members referring to the barge as 'the late lamented', 'I am sorry that the old barge has broken down – it is quite time you had a new one', including the classic comment 'barges seem to be vastly expensive things'.[91] The records show that in 1925 the college 'hired a river steamer from Salter's and had a marquee for teas, whilst using the barge to change from'[92]. A new hull was

The Balliol barge of 1881 photographed in 1969
Oxfordshire County Council Photographic Archive

eventually ordered at a cost of £800, the barge house being deemed reasonably sound with some reconstruction. The total cost with ventilation and drainage improvements was £1,620. Mention of the barge from the 1920s onwards becomes less and less: the perennial question of moving the barge down (to Henley) was mooted in 1950.[93] A further entry of 1957 notes the role of the Bargee or Waterman as being 'responsible for organising the long distance race, dealing with the clubs, punt, property and organising boat club parties, i.e. beer and orgies after dinner' – this is an anonymous quote.[94] By late 1950s Balliol had laid foundations for its purpose-built boathouse and the barge was no longer needed.

The Balliol 'Bargee' of 1959-60, David Kingston, recollects the barge being painted 'slightly pink tinged cream with some red trimmings', with 'a dingy red interior with padded benches along the sides and a long wooden table in the middle'.[95] He also remembers one Eights Week where the rowers were summoned at an ungodly hour from their beds as the Balliol barge had been cut loose during the night and had drifted downstream; she was luckily caught in the Gut. Kingston writes that any practical work was done in his day by the waterman, Ted Holton. Ted, writes Kingston, was a good coach and 'earned some extra money by trying to teach girls from one of the secretarial schools to row'.

Norman Dix, the Univ waterman remembers that the Balliol barge was used by St Catherine's until sold to 'an American' (probably Maccoun) and that 'it went downstream with a man called Tate'; the American disappeared and wasn't heard of for two years.[96] By this time the Balliol barge was, according to Norman, at the bottom of the river. The Thames Conservancy were alerted to Tate. Tate eventually got in touch with the waterman Mike Turk who raised the barge and took her down to her present moorings at Richmond. Turk has done a considerable amount of renovation. The Balliol barge was put up for auction through Phillips at Henley 1996, but was withdrawn at around £100,000, it is believed. The Dean of Balliol in 1998, Dr John Jones, writes that he last saw the barge in 1960, 'a sodden wreck' but went to the Phillips viewing.[97] He noted that the 'old lockers for rowers were still in place' (rabbit hutches with wire grills) but that 'generally restoration had been halted'. Phillips recorded that the barge was reputed to have been designed by Alfred Waterhouse (1830-1905) architect of the Natural History Museum in London (1873-81); there appears to be no documentary evidence to prove this.

THE QUEEN'S COLLEGE BARGES

The Queen's College barge history should be a fuller account than most, as during the period 1860 to 1908 they appear to have owned four barges. However lack of archival evidence at the college dramatically foreshortens the story; Norman Dix believes that the records all 'went in the dustbin' around the late 1930s.[98]

Sherwood writes that 'Queen's College ... since about 1860 had one of the City barges' which was the old City barge, i.e. the Lord Mayor's barge; he prints a plate in his book *Oxford Rowing* of 1900.[99] It is a massive structure with a great ornate prow, an upper deck possibly with seating; the round-headed windows appear to be divided by pilasters and a decorated lower architrave appears close to the hull. Nicholls Palmer confirms that this 'has the appearance of the City or Lord Mayor's Barge – with arms on the stern very like the city arms'. The carving too apparently shows similarities to the model of the last City barge in the Museum of London. OUBC *Captain's Books* lodged at the Bodleian note that on March 9th 1863 'Trinity bumped Wadham at the Queen's barge' which may well be the first surviving mention of the barge, should no further documents be found at the college.[100].

Richard Norton's appendix to Nicholls Palmer's book notes that 'the last true Lord Mayor's barge was sold in 1860 and then served as the Queen's College Barge until 1872 ...'.[101] The second barge commissioned by the college was apparently built in this year according to Sherwood. Norton writes that in 1885 Queen's bought the Skinners' barge from Balliol, being 'well past its prime'.[102] There is a photograph of the city barge with round-headed windows in the Centre for Oxfordshire Studies.

The fourth barge was commissioned in 1908 and is still

The Oriel and Queen's barges
W. Sherwood, Oxford Rowing

The Queen's barge – Eights Week *c.*1890s – Oriel to the left
Oxfordshire County Council Photographic Archive

afloat at Binsey being owned by Richard Hamel-Cooke, an undergraduate in the 1970s. He lived on the barge during 1978-79 and eventually bought it from Lucy Smith, the granddaughter of Sir John Smith, founder of the Landmark Trust (Sir John also restored the Jesus College barge)[103]. The Queen's barge is now used as a houseboat. Lisa Harker, a social affairs advisor for the BBC, lived on board as a tenant in the early part of 1998. The barge resting near Port Meadow, is really quite enchantingly converted to a houseboat, complete with mains water, electricity, central heating, washing machine, super loo, a splendid bath on a raised dais, and commodious sitting room with fireplace and wood burning stove. A resident mink plays away below the hull. The old flagpole is still there, as is the eagle to the prow. An earlier interior in the *Oxford Times* photographic archive shows a somewhat sparse 1950s interior.

Norman Dix, Univ's waterman, recounts a story of the Queen's barge having trouble negotiating the Osney Bridge,

The interior of the Queen's barge *c.* 1950s
By courtesy of The Oxford Times

the headroom being only 7'. Apparently her bilges were filled with water to lower the superstructure, a somewhat dangerous exercise, and successfully pumped out after clearing the bridge. Norman, who remembers a Polish man owning her at one point, calls the barge 'an unusual steel plate job', her steel hull having been integrated to her superstructure. A photograph of the 1920s shows the somewhat lineal plainness of fenestration relieved by some ornate scroll-work at the entrance, an elegantly raised prow and delicate iron railings.

Queens College appears to be the last college to purchase a livery barge and therefore closes the early history of the Oxford college barges. However this is only the beginning of the story. New College and Brasenose amongst others were to follow hot foot on the heels of the livery barges, by commissioning 'new generation barges' from Salter's, who were firmly established as barge builders to the colleges.

The Queen's barge of 1908
The Oxfordshire County Council Photographic Archive photograph c. *1920s*

The Brasenose College Barges

Brasenose Boat Club records start at the beginning of the nineteenth century; a *Minutes Book* of 1815-36 notes the college as head of the river in 1815. A later volume dated 1837 makes excellent reference to the Procession Night of 1845 (see p. 14). Brasenose again took the head and celebrated with 'a bumps supper which would have made the hair of any modern vice principal stand on end'.

Sherwood writes that the OUBC's original barge may have been used by Brasenose after 1846, although there is no evidence for this in the college records.[104] The first reference to a Brasenose barge appears to be in the *Minutes Book* of 1837-72 concerning the Torpids Race of 1857, 'a well contested race, most gallantly rowed by our crews, ended in bumping Balliol opposite our barge'.[105] A second entry of 1860 writes that 'Brasenose after a splendid race ran into University at the Brasenose Barge.'[106] 1862 shows another entry: 'Brasenose were of course received at the Barge with loud cheers', the barges being an important morale-raising platform for the rowers. W.B.Woodgate's sporting history mentions his being on the Brasenose barge in 1863.[107] Boat Club accounts of 1860 indicate £40 paid to Salter's in 1861 which was repeated annually with variances up to £60, from that year to 1866; it is not clear whether this was rental or maintenance. In 1862 George West, a boatman was paid £9 for 'alterations' and further repairs later in the year. After 1873 the bills appear be mainly those of George West, representing about £25-£35 a term. The committee minutes of 1862 record his wages to be £12-15 per annum. Small necessities include bills for marmalade debited at 13s 6d and Powells for a bath for the barge, printing barge tickets and a new raft in February 1880.[108]

An early photograph of 1876 shows the first Brasenose barge, which was removed to Medley in 1882.

The Brasenose barge 1876
By kind permission of the Principal and Fellows of the Kings's Hall and College of Brasenose, Oxford.

This is of clapperboard construction to the superstructure with a small deck aft, its fenestration being of three square sashes with a small square at the prow and one door. It appears to be of plain design probably typical of the barges for hire at that time.

In January and February 1881 a committee met to 'consider the advisability of raising a fund for the purpose of paying Salter's bill and building a new barge'. Circulars were distributed in true Oxonian manner. By October 'discussions on the condition of the Barge Fund' and steps to be taken for ordering the new barge were afoot. By January 23rd Salter had (graciously) consented to take £300 in payment of this account – the motion was carried that 'Salter's tender be accepted' for the new barge. Apart from these records there is a solicitor's bill from Thomas Davenport in connection with the 1882 barge, although little other documentary evidence appears.[109]

An entry in the Boat Club minutes mentions that a new chimney was erected on the barge by Browns of Cornmarket Street in the Lent Term of 1889; a note indicating that extensive repairs had been carried out twice since are all that remains.

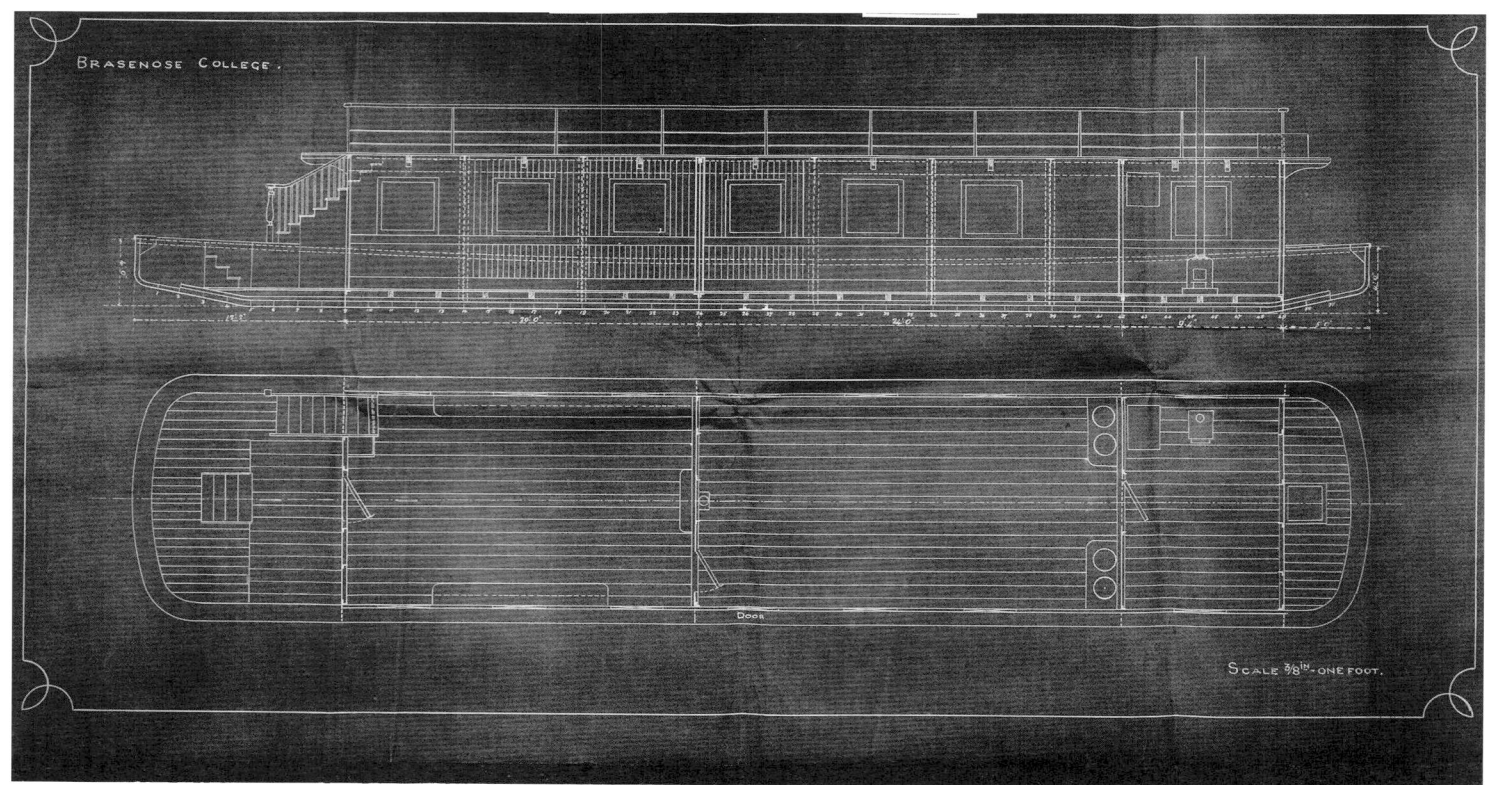

Blueprints of the third Brasenose College barge
By kind permission of the Principal and Fellows of the King's Hall and College of Brasenose, Oxford

By October 1925 'a new college barge ha[d] become an urgent necessity'. A senior fellow, Mr Stocker, made a 'munificent gift' of £2,000; this was added to the old member's appeal fund, Oxford's fail-safe fund raising method. A note records that the third barge 'may carry on the traditions of the past'. There are blue prints in the college records.[110]

A small photograph from the Principal Stallybrass' unrivalled photographic collection shows the barge, taken in 1929. Brasenose is a college with a strong rowing tradition; they did much to engender and preserve the college barges by their usage of three generations of the genre.

Rowntree, writing an article dated July 1956, defending the barge tradition at Oxford and attacking the modernist boathouses, believed the Brasenose barge to be at Chertsey 'painted yellow and black'. In the 1960s it was moored at Littlemore. Norman Dix remembers that the last Brasenose barge went to Abingdon for the Sea Scouts and notes that 't'wixt wind and water she got so thin she went down'. Fortuitously new information has come to light in 2001.

The Brasenose barge still lives, now known as 'Baycraft' and moored at the Henley Rowing Club upstream from Leander advertising itself as 'a floating activity and residential base for young people.' It was run by the Berkshire Association of Youth Clubs who took possession of the barge in 1952 when it was moored at Abingdon and was then known as *The Mary Watson*. Similarly to other barges, it was vandalised and eventually taken on by the Twyford Round Table who took her to Henley where a berth was provided by the town council. Some restoration work was undertaken by a group called the Dolphin Voyagers and since 1991 the Berkshire Association of Young People has been responsible for raising funds for her upkeep, through a band of volunteers.

The Christ Church Barge

Christ Church most definitely 'had a barge' according to Sherwood; this is corroborated by the OUBC *Captain's Books* at the Bodleian.[111] In the Torpids racing of 1857 it was noted 'Oriel bumped Worcester at the Christ Church barge' (this could well be an earlier barge to that mentioned by

The third Brasenose barge
Photograph from the Stallybrass Collection taken in 1929
By kind permission of the Principal and Fellows of the King's Hall and College of Brasenose, Oxford

Sherwood). Unfortunately the college have no material on their barge although a good picture exists in the National Monuments Record Office. A small publication written by R. Frost on the *Christ Church Boat Club* states that the Boat Club probably existed as early as 1817. Frost mentions the fees in 1861 for entrance to the Boat Club as 'being three guineas for a nobleman', two for a 'Gentleman commoner' and 'other members of the House' one guinea. He also writes that Christ Church took their barge to Henley in 1907 'to provide luncheons, teas and a social meeting place'.

Judith Curthoys, Christ Church's archivist, writes that the 'first reference to the barge is in 1866 when it is noted as a destination for a practice outing. There are notes of the barge being varnished and having new planks installed, of it being towed to Henley for the regatta and of Salter's towing it away for overhaul' but little else of interest. [112] Christ Church, who own the Meadow, were the first college to build a boat house in 1939.

The Christ Church barge *c.* 1902
The National Monuments Record Office

The Pembroke College Barges

Pembroke appears to be the next college chronologically to mention a barge. The OUBC *Captain's Records* of 1855-70 on the Torpids of March 1870 write that 'Balliol (bumped) Pembroke opposite the Pembroke Barge'.[113] Sherwood noted that Pembroke shared a barge above Salter's with New College, St John's and Jesus after 1877; perhaps by this time the first barge's life was over. Although the college do not have records to confirm either of these claims (the archive materials are scarce from 1855-90) it appears irrefutable that Pembroke did have use of a barge at this date. The *Pembroke College Boat Club Records* of 1881 make the first mention in college records of the barge: 'a race from Claspers to the Pembroke Barge' is recorded.[114]

A committee meeting, simply dated 1882, indicates the merging of the Boat Club and Barge accounts. It announces 'no member of the Boat Club may row or steer from the Pembroke Barge who does not subscribe to Salter for the year or term' (a

The 1903 Pembroke College barge *c.* 1960s
By kind permission of the Master and Fellows of Pembroke College, Oxford

daily fee of 1/6d was allowed for the uncommitted). The accounts were read and passed but were not very satisfactory since 'the barge had been painted, new blinds and table covers [provided] inside'. That the barge was painted in this year would indicate an earlier building date, it would be unlikely that it would need painting a year after its inauguration.

A committee meeting of April 1883 notes the election of Mr Nicholetts as 'bargee' whose duties included 'collector of subscriptions'. A few years later in June 1891 the committee sanctioned £50 from the reserve fund to repairs on the barge and commissioned Mr Moore, 'architect of Beaumont Street' to employ Castle, presumably a builder to do the work. No further evidence comes to light until the year 1900 when the Boat Club were 'worried by the age and unsound condition of the college barge', a statement which again would tend to confirm an early building date, as twenty years would hardly be deemed old in boat-building terms. A Barge Fund was set up; the estimated cost of £800 was bandied to members on a printed circular who generously responded with around half the suggested price.

Boat Club Records indicate that in the Michaelmas Term of 1903 they received 'Messrs Salter's bill for the new barge together with the architect's fee', although tantalisingly no mention is made of his name. Messrs Moohie and Ward were given the order for upholstery and in the summer term a flag was given to the barge by R. Sanbury. A post war reference of the Hilary Term 1919 notes that 'with very few students back, ten attended at the barge' from which somewhat disturbingly an Eight had to be picked for Torpids.

H. Longuet-Higgins writes of the barge in the *Pembroke College Record* of 1963-4; he bemoans the loss of this 'stalwart old vessel', recalling the sunny days of the turn of the century when the Pembroke barge was a rendezvous 'for pretty frocks, wonder hats and parasols'. He remembers the barge as 'quite the prettiest in the whole line' its oeil de boeuf windows showing remarkable likeness to those of the Keble barge of the same date.[115] He similarly recalls the barge's great adventure to Henley in 1906 where she 'squeezed through locks, with some damage' never to return there. He remembered a 'bucklunch' served aboard on Ladies Day where the barge, complete with awning 'made the perfect

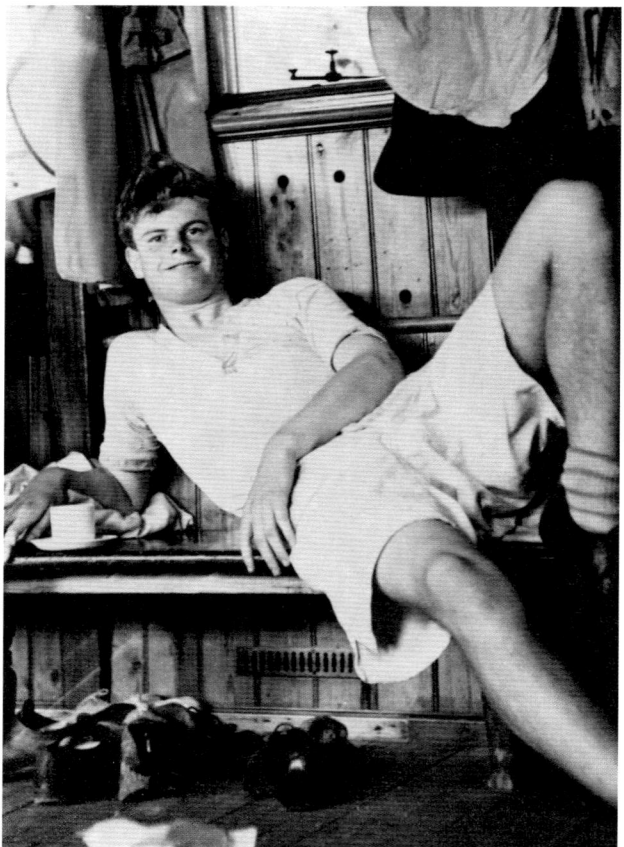

Unknown oarsman – most probably in the Dressing Room
By kind permission of the Master and Fellows of Pembroke College, Oxford

clubhouse'. Memories too, he recalls, of Dolph Talboys, waterman at the turn of the century and lastly East, with 'paintpot, screwdriver, shovel, baling can and barge pole', the essential accoutrements for the college waterman. Lesley East's daughter recalls wonderful family picnics on the barge when term had ended and days spent happily playing there. Norman Dix, the Univ waterman remembers being asked by East to pump the barge every day as she was leaking badly. The Captain of Boats came down and took over from Norman. Apparently in less than ten days she was in ten foot of water. Len Andrews, brother of the Exeter boatman remembers that she started to go down the night after Summer Eights; Norman believes she was towed to Salter's in 1964 as she was sinking fast; and here she was probably broken up. Norman has memories of some very fine cast iron railings with the roses of the Pembroke College arms on them being loaded onto a scrap lorry.

THE WORCESTER COLLEGE BARGE

The Worcester College barge is a bit of an enigma; the college have no records of her, but the gallant Sherwood does make mention of her: 'in 1871 Worcester moved to a small barge behind Queen's and gave an annuity to an old woman to her death for the barge'. The barge was to be theirs when she died, a protracted arrangement which was eventually finalised in 1900. Roger Hutchin's account of rowing at Magdalen College, *Well Rowed Magdalen*, shows a plan of the position of the barges in 1935 in which the Worcester barge is placed in between Corpus and the Talboys raft.[116]

Norman Dix, the Univ waterman remembers her being 'not very big' and to Len Andrews she seemed to be the 'shape of a punt'; both agree that she was broken up at Salter's, consumed with rot.

THE NEW COLLEGE BARGES

The indomitable Sherwood informs us that in the 1880s New College shared a barge above Salter's along with Pembroke, St John's and Jesus; this was the 'labelled' barge named above its windows, access being only available through the fenestration.[117] Norton writes that this barge was owned by King's, the boat builders.

No mention is made of this in the New College archives, which date their first barge from the year 1879. The only reference to this first barge was sent in by an old member, Michlam, and is a letter to Mr Salter dated 13th February 1878 'indicating the best measurements for a new barge, a saloon of 27', dressing room of 21' with an overall (recommended) length of 62' and width of 12 feet'. The hull was to be about the same as the University barge, built the year before. It was to be dressed with four windows to the saloon and three to the dressing room. It is believed this barge was used later by Merton College. This shows a pretty barge attractively decorated with a series of three sash windows, each set with one wider sash, balanced by two more attenuated counterparts. The glazing bars are worked to represent a centrally placed hexagon, perhaps mirroring the rose motif on the balustrading above. A door, glazed in the same manner, is sited after the first two sets of windows. The stern windows, sitting in what appears to be a rounded section, are simpler casements divided by sturdy pilasters. The overall effect is a barge of considerable lightness in design.

The ensuing reference is many years later and appears in October 1926 when a committee was set up to 'look at the question of the barge', which 'seems beyond repair'.[118] A letter dated 6th November 1926 from C. J. Bridges noted the barge to be 'tipping badly'. Having examined below the floorboards Bridges declared 'her back to be broken'. She had been tied to a tree and weighted, as was common practice during Eights Week, to stop her turning turtle.

Some pencilled notes of the East Boat Building Company, Caversham, Reading, dated November 1926 entitled 'Specification of work in the renovation of the New College Barge' indicate efforts were made to bring her back to life. The 'bottom was good, the roof lets in water and the dressing room shows signs of weakness'. Various remedies were suggested: taking up the floorboards, making good the trellis work, removing the roof, fixing steel joists, along with an interior varnish and exterior paint, all of which Bristow, the writer, deemed would give the barge 'at least another five years of life'. These were really fire-fighting tactics, the roof being made watertight, by covering it with a substance known as rubberoid, until a new barge could be obtained.

Correspondence had been set up between the architect George Drinkwater of 8 Warwick Avenue in 1926 and the College. He wrote 'I shall be pleased to advise you about a new barge and if you wish it design one and get it carried out'. He had at the time designs out to tender for the second Magdalen barge and was keen to promote the merits of a new concrete hull; there was difficulty in obtaining good timber at this time.[119] According to RIBA files George Carr Drinkwater (1880-1941) was an architect/artist but 'better known as a rowing coach and writer on rowing'. He apparently died under enemy action in 1941.

A further letter of 26th December notes 'I think I could design you a barge on simple lines which could be embellished later at £2,000', his fees being the usual architect's charge of 6%. Letters of appeal, the traditional

The Shared Barge
W. Sherwood, Oxford Rowing

Opposite: the New College barge of 1909
By kind permission of the Warden and Fellows of New College, Oxford

boat club fund raising method, were duly dispatched and answers returned with some amusing comments:

'Do you think it wise to provide for the replacement of a Barge by a sinking fund?' [120]

The boatbuilder Thorneycroft was asked to bid for the construction, as were James Taylor and Bates, contractors to the Admiralty War Office and Air Board. James Taylor and Bates of Chertsey won the day at a cost of £1575. The barge was built in their boatyard during 1927-8 and delivered to Oxford in March 1928.

One Cyprian J. Bridge kept an eye on the progress for the college, reporting in a letter dated 2nd December 1927, but a man called Blandford appeared to be in overall charge. By May of the following year the Bursar was writing to the builders with a list of complaints, most especially concerning the condition of the roof and quality of painting. The barge had to be repainted in August 1929 and again in 1933. By the early 1930s Salter's executed repairs to the floor, dressing room and saloon. By the autumn of 1935 dry rot was discovered in the roof and stern, which was rectified. There is a letter from Salter's, dated February 5th 1937, wherein it states they thought 'the hull to be sound but perhaps', rather delicately they suggest that, 'inferior wood had been used in the superstructure'.

Whispers were afoot concerning the possibility of a

The New College barge, Chelsea Reach, 2000

purpose-built boathouse; a note of 1941 somewhat stoically states 'but we must keep the barge till we build the boathouse'. By the early 1950s, when the college had built a new boathouse, letters are on file from those asking about the possibility of living on or acquiring the barge. Raymond Baxter, the well-known broadcaster and traditional boat enthusiast was an interested party at one point. The barge was moored at the mouth of the Cherwell for many years; Salter's are recorded as having quoted £65 to move it in the late 1950s.

A similar proposal was put to the Warden of New College in August 1957; H. Britt, a freshman of Worcester, fancied a spell living on the barge; like many, he found he had a great problem in securing a mooring and had to withdraw his proposal. Eventually an enterprising Mrs Ross of Kensington in 1960 offered a brave £50 and proposed to tow it to London. She eventually purchased it on November 9th and with the aid of the boatman, Harris of Weirs Lane who looked after it for a while, the New College barge left Oxford on her return voyage to London. A letter from Sarah Hosking, who staged an early exhibition of the Oxford College barges, mentions a drawing of the 1927 barge, but it appears this is no longer held in the New College archives.

An advertisement for the barge appeared in *Country Life* in 1972 where she was put up for sale as a 'comfortable and unusual pied a l'eau'. Moored on Cheyne Walk, where she is to this day, she boasted central heating, three bedrooms, bathroom and galley.[121] In the late 1990s she was owned by William Meredith Owen and rented out. Her upper construction is of clapperboard; she still maintains the distinctive fenestration and pilasters with a large heavily-paned square window to her stern. Her paintwork is of burgundy and cream with gold finishings. Some rather large pineapple finials now crown her upper railings.

THE CORPUS CHRISTI COLLEGE BARGES

Corpus Christi appears to follow New College in the growing band of barge enthusiasts. An article published in 1905 mentions that 'the college barge was built twenty one years ago (*c.* 1884) at a cost of £600'.[122] The amount was raised by various means, notably a capitation tax and debentures of £25, the sum loaned being paid off by 1892. Sherwood writes that Corpus 'had a room at Hall's [barge], and took on the University College barge'. Mrs Butler, the Corpus Christi archivist, can find no reference in the *Captain's Books* of 1872-6 of the Merchant Taylors' or the University College barge being used by Corpus Christi.[123] An earlier entry dated October 1870 describes a college meeting held on 26th October to 'determine whether the college should have a dressing room at Salter's', the motion being unanimously carried. This appears to be the full extent of information on the first Corpus Christi barge, bar one exciting discovery of a fine pencil drawing in delicate condition protected by an ageing brown envelope in the Corpus Christi archives, marked 'T.G. Jackson'.[124]

A photograph, taken in 1906, hangs on the staircase of the Corpus Christi archives. A shallow hull supports a pleasantly-proportioned house structure, decorated with five great oval windows, with casement openings; these are intersected by simple pilasters. A more diminutive oval sits in the clapper-boarded stern. The flagpole and pelican figurehead are found to the fore of the boat; interestingly an iron frame has been erected on the forward deck, presumably to make use of further covered space should the weather be bad. On the upper deck an array of boaters and extravagantly behatted ladies sit on the benches, protected by the wooden railings.

The similarities between the drawing and the finished article are notable. Little was altered except the configuration of the stern; this was extended to balance the length of the bow, with changes to the stern window. The oval fenestration, being the major design feature, appears to have been finer and more attenuated in the drawing; it also appears that Jackson had intended the whole frame to open, as opposed to the executed two casements. Slightly more architectural embellishment, such as scroll work terminating at either side of the fenestration appears to have been omitted. The design of the balustrading and staircase appear from the photograph to be much as the architect intended. Internally the barge was to have a double sliding door, seats to either side of the main saloon with boiler and stove placed on the end saloon wall. Six basins and a W.C. took up the washroom space to the stern of the craft.

The Corpus Christi barge *c.* 1906
By kind permission of the President and Fellows of Corpus Christi College, Oxford

William Whyte, a post graduate student at Wadham researching the work of Jackson, writes that 'the enlargement of the windows and the note explaining it are undoubtedly in Jackson's hand'.[125] He believes other writing on the drawing to be that of an assistant, as is the design itself. However the initial idea and rough sketch 'would have been by Jackson himself'. Whyte confirms this by a note he found in the *Oxford Magazine*:[126]

The New Corpus barge has taken its place in the 'world famed line of floating palaces' on the river. Those who expected that it would add to the beauty of Isis will be disappointed. It compares favourably, it is true, with one of its neighbours, but the experiment of placing a cabman's shelter on a raft was not likely to be repeated and the Corpus barge has at least some of the lines of a boat. Its main fault is the size

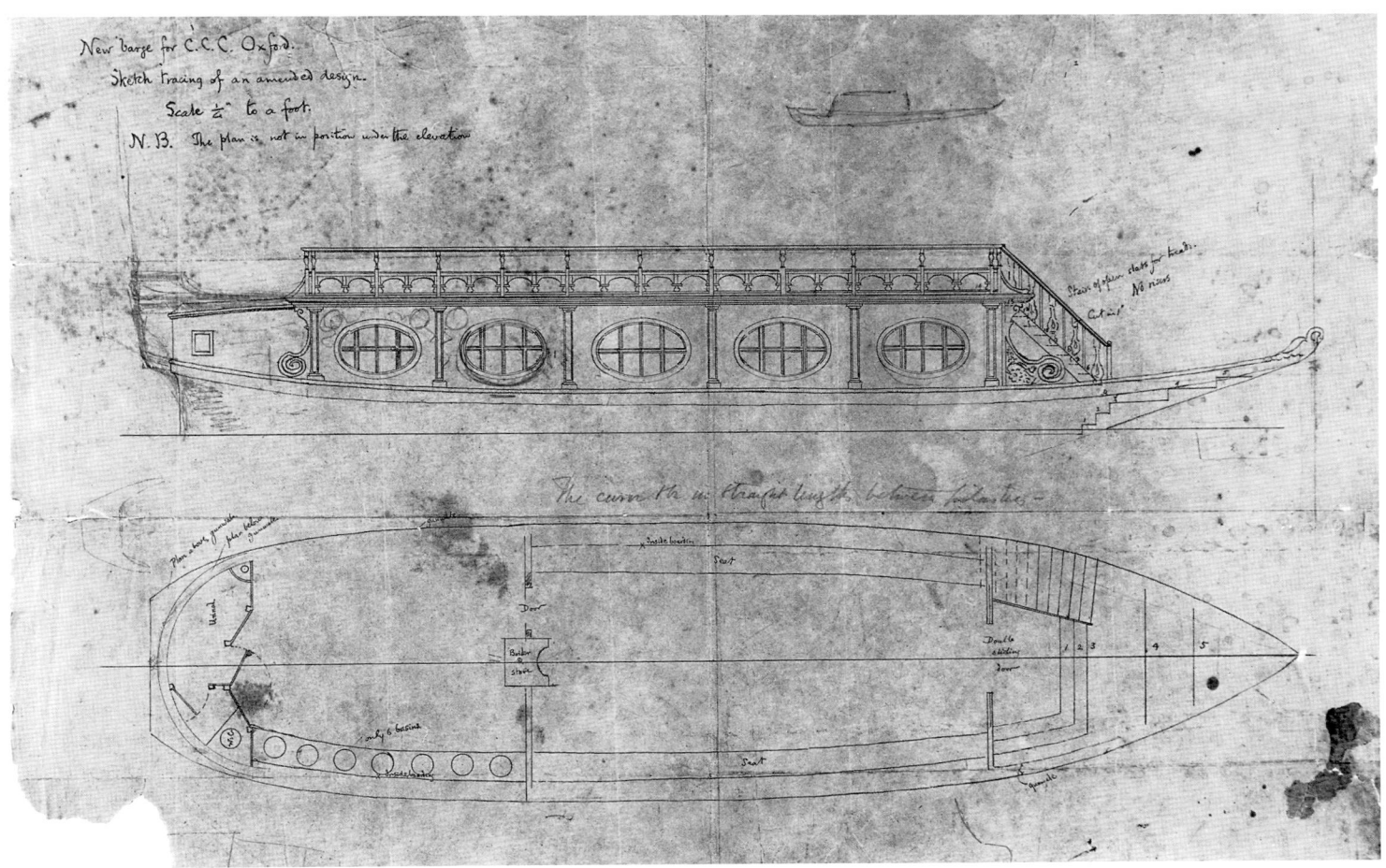

T.G. Jackson's drawing of the Corpus barge
By kind permission of the President and Fellows of Corpus Christi College, Oxford

of its windows: their shape, we are told, was designed by Mr Jackson, the architect, while their size was increased to provide the Corpus crews with an easier ingress and exit than was calculated any door could afford.

Repairs are known to have been executed *c.* 1905, to the roof and interior costing £50, but apart from that no further mention is made in the college records of the Jackson barge.

The second Corpus Christi barge was a memorial barge donated in memory of the Reverend Joseph Hooper Maude (1871-5) and Louis Edward Joseph Maude (1910-14) the latter 'last seen wounded during the first Battle of the Somme in 1916', being described as 'very cheerful' at the time.[127] It was to a great extent built as a replica of the first, following the tradition of its particularly distinctive oval window openings. Described as 'true and faithful sons of Corpus' by Mrs Maude and Dr Cecily Maude, it was 'to fix a last glimpse of Louis, so characteristic of both him and his father

The Second Corpus Christi barge, *c.* 1930s
By kind permission of the President and Fellows of Corpus Christi College, Oxford

that the happy inspiration of a memorial barge' took shape.[128]

A letter records the acknowledgement of an architects' certificate and cheque for £100 sent to him, the architect being F. M. Harrison, whose talent was mentioned in the Captain's speech on the opening day of the barge.[129]

This shows a bulkier image than the 1884 barge, which probably made far better use of boat space. The 'Jackson' windows, now the hallmark of the Corpus barges, are configured in a series of seven, broken after a pair to either end by a set of French doors, with a central section of three ovals. The stern sports three rectangular casements and at the bow the elegantly-poised pelican, the Corpus emblem[130], stands as a figure-head, its bowed neck seemingly echoing the line of the bow. Sturdy double columns support the overhang from the upper decking. This is protected by wooden railings, the lower portion of which are decorated by rectangular shields bearing the college arms and presumably those of the Maude family.

A further letter in the Maude file at Corpus Christi from N. W. Harrison FRIBA. 'thanks the President for his approval for the design of the carvings of the barge'.[131] Meticulous notes from President Allen, dated 4th February 1929, record that the barge was constructed of elm with oak below the water and that the railings were to be, 'like the Pembroke barge'. There was to be an armchair and a Chesterfield, space for pictures and charts, a flagpole and staircase. The interior was to be of plain matchboarding, not teak or oak (which he underlines) in the 'insistence of economy'. Perhaps it is partly due to Allen's fastidious supervision of the construction that the barge is preserved to this day.

The opening of the new barge described as 'attractive and comfortable' took place on May 7th 1930 and was a splendid affair with a lunch laid on at the college for fifty and 'one hundred and fifty assembled for the presentation'.

> The skill of the builder Mr Salter and his men, the patience of the committee and the ingenuity of George were all amply praised.[132] A tablet was put up over the fireplace to commemorate the donors and the two Maudes in whose memory the barge stood. *The Record* continues 'that after lunch guests made their way down to the riverbank where, amid much applause the barge was unlocked by Miss Maude, sister of Joseph, who had earlier been presented with the key.

The barge was recorded as the 'heroine of the occasion', being 'subjected to a severe test of buoyancy', her upper decks being laden with supporters, as the photograph shows.

There is a letter from Salter's, dated April 12th 1932, sending a drawing of the Maude coat of arms to the family. It mentions 'a small box containing plaster patterns including two of each of three different brass castings of ornamentations on the railing of the new Corpus Christi barge' – (the Maude coat of arms shows a lion rampant on black, white and red stripes). It appears great care was taken during the consultation process with the donors of the barge.

Little further reference to the barge exists until an inventory of the barge, dated 21st March 1943, included a water purifier, weighing machine, roll of coconut matting, seat cushions, cane chairs, flag tablecloth, fire fender, coal bucket and pictures. The Corpus Christi barge was, as others, requisitioned under the emergency powers on 13th July of that year by the Admiralty 'for naval purposes'. In 1953 the *College Record* states that even with the pressure of purpose-built boathouses ever present the 'barge is not beyond our means'. However that year marked the agreement with New College for Corpus Christi to share a purpose-built boathouse. The Corpus Christi barge triumphantly continues to function to this day as a college annexe.

The annual report in *The Pelican* of 1983-4, written by Dr Charles Edward, a Jesus College professor and the senior member in charge of clubs, stated that the 'Corpus Barge has been in the care of the Trust for the Preservation of Oxford College Barges for some years,' and that 'great inroads' were being made to rescue and restore her. Robert Maccoun, the Canadian maritime engineer, was instrumental in the rebirth of this ageing vessel. His scheme to slip the 1930 Corpus Commemoration barge into a steel hull, thus creating an envelope around the existing wooden one, was a success. The complicated exercise took place in the Kidney Stream on the east side of the Isis just above Donnington Bridge where the barge is moored today. Lady Wheare, an avid committee woman, whose husband was Master of Exeter College, suggested the setting up of a trust for the preservation of the barges. The idea came to her one evening when she met Sarah Hoskings who was setting up an exhibition about the barges. The trust with Bernard Fagg of the Pitt Rivers Museum as its

Presentation photograph – the Corpus Christi College barge, 1930
By kind permission of the President and Fellows of Corpus Christi College, Oxford

first Chairman was active in saving the Hertford, Jesus and Corpus Christi College barges.[133] A report of the Trust dated 24th May 1971 notes that thirteen barges were in existence at that time, the Jesus barge restored in 1969, and the Hertford's superstructure rebuilt after fire damage in 1969. They highlight the Univ, St John's and Corpus Christi as vessels worth preserving. Sub-committees were set up but it appears they battled against poor funding, amongst other problems. Interestingly this report recommends the setting up of a Museum of Rowing and the River with the idea of housing it on the barges at Oxford. Their concept has perhaps materialised as The River and Rowing Museum at Henley, which is now open to the public.

Lady Wheare tells how she was sent off by Maccoun, with no real knowledge of boats, to inspect and buy a steel hull for the Hertford barge. The boatyard laid out sheets for her to lie on whilst, clad in a white suit, she examined the hull for holes. Some of the work for the Trust was by all accounts frustrating; Maccoun was a 'hands on man' who wanted to do all the work himself.

Corpus, whilst handing the barge over to the Trust, retained the rights for three students to live on the barge, the income contributing towards its maintenance. At the end of 1997 four students lived on board. Jonathan Prag in his fourth year stood guard and spent Christmas on the barge, it being a condition of their tenure that she is not left unattended. The original railings were taken down in the 1990s and no longer exist, except for a set rather poignantly used as a garden fence to a neighbouring boat. Recently, extensive repair work has been undertaken. She is truly a students' barge, now the only real barge used by a college, as the photograph below reveals:

The 1930s plaque by the door names the architect, Nathaniel William Harrison FRIBA, the boatbuilder John Henry Salter and John Dobson, his foreman of works. College blades, draped classical statuary, posters and 'vin de table' lamps make up a student bedsit of sizeable and stylish proportions. The 1955 registration plate shows the barge's length to be 70'8". The main saloon houses a kitchen to the prow, with a large ship's cabin to the stern, complete with comfortable old bed on a raised dais for the captain. Her exterior is painted a mustardy colour and seems to blend with the surroundings, so much so that many hardly notice her as they pass by on the Thames. Complete with electricity and telephone camouflaged by willows she is a veritable junior water rat's refuge.[134]

The Corpus Christi barge – interior December 1997

The Jesus College Barges

Jesus College followed Corpus Christi in engendering the college barge tradition. Sherwood writes that they shared a barge with New College and St John's in the late 1870s but that their first recorded ownership was not until 1887.[135] However a document issued by T. G. Tagg and Son is in the archives, dated December 14th 1884. This shows an estimate and rough drawing of 'a proposal for a college barge at a very low price – it will be plain but well built, the hull will be of good build, a good deck and the roof [always a problem] laid with our patent caulking seam', ensuring a 'tight deck'. The college presumably chewed this over and by 1887 a contract was issued from Tagg, dated 20th April 1887 with an estimate of £347.30, including extras of 'circular heads to windows, twelve new lockers, flagstaff and table'. This agreement was ratified by a solicitor's bill, dated November 28th 1887 for £1 16s from J. J. Bickerton which reads: 'to conferring and advising as to contract for building the Jesus College Boat Club Barge for £325'. Notes indicate the college had looked at the old Magdalen College barge but deemed it too expensive to repair.[136]

Tagg's patent caulking system was not as waterproof as he perhaps would have believed and was to cause problems highlighted in a letter dated 5th May 1897 to Mr Hawke Hughes of Jesus College. Tagg assured Hughes 'that a slight leakage is no worry and was to be expected in a new craft of that description' (all timber craft take in a little water, to the uninitiated this can prove somewhat disturbing). He advises, as has many a boatbuilder, that the 'wood soon swells and prevents further leakage' suggesting the college 'swill down the decks everyday in the summer as on a yacht's deck'.

A college circular was sent out to old members at the beginning of 1887 urging them to donate; undergraduates and graduates contributed the remainder needed. The Reverend Hughes donated £109 which, in economic terms, seems to have saved the day. A list of purchases for the barge survives including a stove, Baycock cushions, matting, a raft and printed stationary for the barge, giving some concept of the creature comforts on board.

The original plans indicated a somewhat hazardous spiral staircase. Internally there was, as in all the barges, a main saloon, 9'2" x 13', with seats and lockers, an adjoining cloakroom being splendidly equipped with five basins and lavatory. Notes suggest that the 14'-15' at bow and stern, a legacy of the livery barge composition, was later deemed for college purposes a 'wasted space'.

April 1887 marks, in accounting terms, the first reference to the barge: the insurance being secured by the Phoenix Insurance Company for twelve shillings.[137] Painting in that year is listed as costing £1 2s 6d and ten guineas respectively. Later records list the minutiae of everyday maintenance: 'one mop for Mr Smart for barge and one small brush, an allowance for washing of towels, coals, raft, and pumps', the latter being a truly vital piece of machinery to any barge.[138] The rental from Christ Church for use of the meadow and mooring was £5 per annum. A new chimney was fitted in 1892 and four new blinds. A later entry in the *Boat Club Accounts* indicates that in the Hilary and Trinity terms of 1894 the college agreed to rent the Green Barge, (eventually owned by Salter's according to Norman Dix), during the Pairs races for £1 5s.[139]

Rumblings from Hawkes Hughes dated December 1887, in shaky hand, indicate that he was not personally responsible for the debt and that the roof was still a problem, possibly due to poorly seasoned wood, similar to the New College barge. The indomitable Hawkes however was not to be outdone; the second generation Jesus College barge was more than a figment of his imagination when a circular was issued to old members with the purpose of creating a new barge fund, the

Opposite: the second Jesus College barge
By kind permission of the Principal, Fellows and Scholars of Jesus College, Oxford and The Independent newspaper

old barge being 'in a bad state with its hull absolutely rotten.'

A bill is extant dated 19th October 1911 from John H. England of 68 Abingdon Road, Oxford to W.H. Hughes, Senior Bursar, for the sum of £20 'for preparing plans and supervising of the building of the New Barge for Jesus College Boat Club.' According to the college archivist, Dr Brigid Allen, England was the son of the college architect being particularly influenced by the Arts and Crafts movement. Apparently England borrowed plans of the Trinity and Pembroke barge to help with his plans; these were lent by Salter's, who built the barge. The estimate given by Salter's was £885, the total cost being fairly concluded at £940 14s 8d.

This shows a barge with a somewhat over-emphasised raised and squared stern of clapperboard construction in the galleon manner, being a little similar to that of St John's College. A series of differing window types provides variety in three wide and round-headed sashes divided by pilasters, intersected by French doors with their upper parts glazed. These are followed by what appear to be five sets of full length plainer casements, divided again by pilasters. Open balustrading on the greater part of the deck is balanced by the enclosed portion of the box-like stern.

The Boat Clubs Amalgamated Account for 1914 shows that in May of that year chairs, cards, pistols and brandy were taken to the barge, and the normal tea-making paraphernalia brought down during Eights Week. There is little other accounting evidence, apart from Salter's 1928 bill for new cloth of strong flax canvas and 858' of matchboarding. Additionally new longitudinal beams in the dressing room, some new floor joists and grating over the windows, including an exterior paint of white lined with green, constituted what must have been quite an extensive refurbishment for the barge. In 1953 £800 was spent on further repairs. A note of 7th June 1962 confirms that the University Canoe Club had bought the barge, it was noted that it almost sank in this year.

By 1967-8 John Smith M.P. for Maidenhead, had bought the barge and was discussing its future mooring including sewage disposal plans with Teddington Council. Maccoun's drawings and calculations are in the Jesus College archives.[140] The restoration took place at Tough's Teddington boatyard whose many bills are deposited in the college archives. These accounts came thick and fast during 1968-9. The teak hull was replaced but

Plans of the Jesus College barge 1887
By kind permission of the Principal, Fellows and Scholars of Jesus College, Oxford

the superstructure retained. Smith was amply aided by Robert Maccoun, the restorer and go-between of the barges in their new found roles. Phillip Jebb ARIBA of 140 Sloane Street SW1 prepared a specification dated 24th October 1967, 'as directed and agreed by Mr R. Maccoun', for extensive renovation and refit of the barge including repair of the balustrade, removing gutters, laying a new timber foredeck and stern platform, a new flagpole and figurehead and glazed windows. Maccoun's notes estimate the restoration of the barge to be roughly to the tune of £5,500. Dimensions he recorded note the barge to be 60' in length with 6" L.O.A.; there were even plans to fit a rudder. Quotes from Bossom and Tough varied from £4,600 to £6,650.

In the 1980s the barge returned to Christ Church meadows under the auspices of the Trust for the Preservation of Oxford College barges. Fires and the barges seem at times to go hand in hand; the Dragon barge was virtually destroyed. Norman Dix recalls Peter Bailey, the Keble waterman, getting a call that the Jesus barge was coming back to Oxford; the dilemma was where to put her and also what to do with her. She was, according to Norman, tied up to old piles but was sadly burnt out within a fortnight. The London boatbuilders Turks rescued her from a watery grave, this being amply recorded in the press and *Oxford Today*. [141] She was moored in the spring of 1998 at Turk's London base in Richmond, still painted in green and gold livery with her fiery red dragon proudly protecting her prow.

The Jesus College barge sinking *c.* 1940s
Courtesy of The Oxford County Newspaper

The Magdalen College Barges

Magdalen and Jesus College's barges both seemed to have appeared on the river in 1887. Various archival sources are available concerning the barges at Magdalen College. The earliest appears to be a circular letter of January 1886 indicating 'that a memorial ought to be raised to the late senior Tutor and Estates Bursar, T.H.T. Hopkins'; thus the first Magdalen barge was in fact a memorial barge in similar spirit to the Corpus Christi barge of 1930.[142] The same letter notes that, prior to 1886, a barge was rented by the Boat Club. Peter Fullerton, Treasurer to the Friends of the Magdalen College Boat Club recounts that the College rented a barge from Salter's.[143] *The OUBC Captain's Book* in the Bodleian Library states that on May 17th 1873 in the third race 'Exeter (made a fourth bump) at the Magdalen Barge', this was presumably an earlier rented barge.[144] Sherwood interestingly writes that Magdalen were the 'last to make use of Salter's barge up to 1873' so the dates would appear to tally.[145]

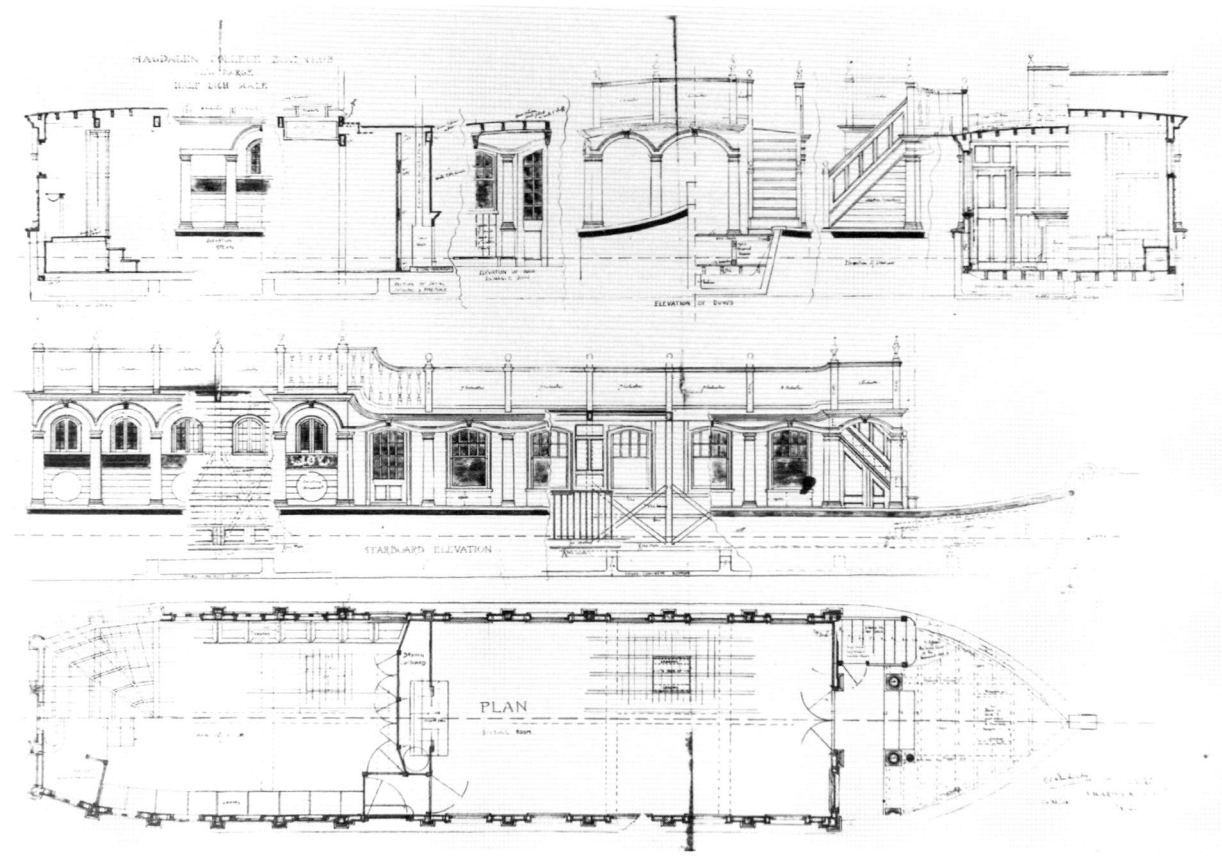

Plan and elevation of the Magdalen College barge
By kind permission of Mouchel International and the President and Fellows of Magdalen College Oxford

The first Magdalen barge 1887, 'The Laden Barge' *c.* 1888
By kind permission of the President and Fellows of Magdalen College Oxford

In respect of the new barge a further letter of February 18th 1886 mentions that 'the committee have 'resolved to consult an architect' to obtain designs and tenders. Funds obtained rose to £700 (an original estimate of £600 had been proposed). In November 1886 the committee requested Mr P.E. Warren 'to prepare designs for a barge', (which were approved) and 'to arrange tenders for carrying them out'. It has been suggested that this barge was designed by Lutyens but there is no documentary evidence to support this. The lowest tender of £800 was accepted but it was decided not to sacrifice certain parts of the design in the interests of economy. The barge was complete by 31st March 1887 and a brass plaque erected to the memory of Tovey Hopkins. This is in fact known by virtue of a letter of complaint indicating that the plaque had been removed many years later.[146]

Sadly there appears to be no further material on the first barge; it is recorded in *Well Rowed Magdalen*, a comprehensive history of Magdalen College Boat Club, as having been demolished around 1925. Sherwood writes that Wadham took on the old Magdalen College barge in 1887; sadly no archival evidence exists to substantiate Sherwood's statement.[147]

In 1927 Magdalen College went headlong into the twentieth century by ordering their second barge with an innovative ferro-concrete hull. Weighing forty-two tons, it boasted the unique 'hennebrique grid system' being concrete reinforced with a complete meshwork of steel rods. She was 70' overall with a 15' beam, and had walls with a thickness of 42". (Len Andrews, the boatman recalls being able to crawl in the great void under the floorboards of the barge). Original plans and elevations are in L.G. Mouchel and Partners' archives, now trading as Mouchel International, who were the engineers responsible for the construction of ferro-concrete floating buildings and vessels at the time.

The plans were drawn up and signed by the architect G.C. Drinkwater of 8 Warwick Avenue, whom Norman Dix refers to as 'dear old Drinkwater' and 'his extraordinary barge'. The second volume of Magdalen College Boat Club records notes that 'the barge was constructed from parts of the earlier 1886 barge'; doubts however have been raised whether in fact this was so.[148] The joinery was carried out by Messrs Holloway and Brothers who had 'a fine joinery works' so the superstructure was deemed to be of 'the very best workmanship'. The barge was ready by the summer of 1927.

This was a particularly ornate barge with Romanesque feel; her elegantly raised stern, being glamorously decorated with strong rounded arches supported by columns, into which were fashioned, with elaborate decoration, round but slightly arched casements. Intricate roundels sporting the initial 'W', paying reference to the founder of the college, William Waynflete, were set below a dado of foliate relief. A door and five wide-arched sashes carry the programme to the bow of the craft, linked by a soft wave-like cornice and intersected by bosses finishing at a slightly raised portico. A turned set of railings provides a finishing touch to the elaborate decorative programme below. Such historicist decoration contrasts notably with the modernity of the craft's construction.

The Mouchel archives describe a great boom in ferro-concrete shipbuilding towards the end of the war.[149] The concrete ship *S.S. Armistice*, drawn up to Mouchel's plans, was the 'first British built sea-going concrete ship of 1918'. Its advantages were seen to be 'reliability, strength and satisfactory behaviour'. Lack of good-quality timber after the war had forced manufacturers to look to new and innovative methods of construction. Magdalen College was the first and only college to adopt this novel method for the building of a college barge. Interestingly the Mouchel archivist, George

Opposite: the second Magdalen barge of ferro-concrete construction 1927 – 'Idle sods on top with the girls'
By kind permission of the President and Fellows of Magdalen College, Oxford and Sir Douglas Dodds-Parker

Crabb, recounts that the low centre of gravity of the ferro-concrete construction eliminated the chance of the barge tipping over. The Magdalen barge was 'built on the slips of the British Motor Boat Club at Chiswick by Messrs Holloway and launched on March 7th on a flood tide'. She was to be fitted and handed over at Oxford. The locks were closed over the winter delaying her journey until the spring, leaving Salter's with only one month to fit her out.

The article explains that the barge could not have cleared Abingdon Bridge when completed, which was why she came back to Oxford to be fitted out. Now resting in Streatley, she must, perhaps with more ballast in her, have overcome this problem in later years.

Eventually she was sold in 1946 to Talboys, the boatbuilders and was used for storage. One derogatory remark notes that 'she sweated and was always damp'. However she stands proud today, over seventy years later at the Swan Diplomat Hotel at Streatley, being actively and popularly in use as part of their conference facilities. There are numerous newspaper articles from the 1980s when she was taken for a refit by the Pangbourne firm of Champions, a project started by Mr Newling Ward, Managing Director of Gulliver Hotels, who owned the Swan at the time. When Ward purchased her in 1979 the old barge was sinking with 3' of water inside. She had since the 1960s been mostly used by a couple as a houseboat/summerhouse.

The Magdalen barge, is according to Mrs Jamie Coppen-Gardener of the Swan Diplomat, immensely popular and now sports the emblem of the hotel where the college symbols once stood. Dr Darwall-Smith, Magdalen College's archivist points out that the lily was the motif most prolifically used on the Magdalen College barge. The barge is the only college barge to be truly working a five day week in a commercial sense. The remaining barges are houseboats or rented out spasmodically. Perhaps her 'modern' twentieth-century construction makes her the most adaptable to present day usage.

The Trinity College Barges

The 1888 Trinity College barge appears to be a near contemporary in date to the first Jesus and Magdalen College barges, its appeal being launched in 1887 with completion the following year.

Trinity College Boat Club accounts survive from 1863. In 1864 Salter's were paid £50, with tips of nearly three shillings (by 1865 the gratuities had risen to ten shillings). The first mention of a Trinity barge is in February 1866; this is rented and was described as 'Salter's barge' in a bill for £27. Salter's barge account seesaws from a low of £27 per annum to £81 in 1871. Barge incidentals such as repairing the clock, pumping water, the repair of locks, biscuits, wine, soap, lamp oil, 'Randolph's cook', Jo Tims bringing in water and Mrs Hicks for pistols are included, much as in other college accounts. 'Lowe for barge' appears to be an entry for the boatman; by 1875 'Waxy', presumably another boatman, became an accounting feature. In May 1882 a 'horse for coaching' was itemised; this was ridden up and down the riverbank as a precursor of the present day bicycle. Slatter and Rose provided the students with periodicals and newspapers, a writing case was mended in 1885, a new flag pole erected 1884-5 and new blinds made in 1883 (at a cost of nineteen shillings). The mending of a windowpane is recorded and the workings of the clock seem to have been a regular nuisance. 1887 appears to be the first year fire insurance was paid (4/6d) perhaps precipitated by the broken window-pane of the same year.

An 1887 Appeal letter sent out to old members claims that 'the present barge is old, inconvenient and too small for the increased numbers of the Boat Club'; an additional grumble was voiced that it did not belong to the club, being rented.[150] The cost of a new barge in 1887/8 was estimated around £700, of which undergraduates were asked to contribute collectively not less than £150. Two splendid donations of £100 helped swell the coffers; £650 was raised before the 1st of July 1888. By this time the barge becomes itemised within the accounts, a guinea being paid for its registration on the river.

In April 1889 the Boat Club paid six shillings in advance for seven years fire insurance; presumably they envisaged a firm future for the vessel. Incidentals from this time include dredging round the barge, mending the pump, newspapers, photographs, charts, oil, towels and painting. A boating stage was purchased from Salter's in 1892-3. The Trinity College Boat Club appear to have been an hospitable lot; an item notes 'drink to men painting the barge (with a pencil note 'why?' written in beside). An entry 'cleaning the barge after Henley' in the autumn of 1898 indicates the barge was taken to the Regatta of that year; it was at Henley again in 1906, 1907 and in June 1913. In 1899 one Mr Menzies was hired to look after the barge during Eights Week.

Turn-of-the-century expenses include repairing of the

Salter's rented barge 1867
By kind permission of the President and Fellows of Trinity College, Oxford

gratings, somewhat humorously an entry for 'putting off repairs' in 1900-1, and 'brandy for the barge' in 1913-14. After this date little further information seems to exist save that hearsay has it that eventually the barge was used as a tea room at Shillingford Bridge.[151] The magnificent griffin figurehead, complete with forked tongue and evil eye, was saved by an old member and preserved, before the barge was (believed) to have been burnt out.

In terms of barge recollections, an old member, Keith Topley QC (who matriculated in 1955) recounts being left in a state of disarray one night after having scaled a wall, post-partying. Thinking he could temporarily replace his torn clothing from one of the barges, he ran down to the meadows and climbed into what he believes may have been the Univ barge for a pair of tubbing bags. Much to his horror the strong arm of authority came down on his shoulder and he was led back, somewhat dismally, to college.

The Trinity College barge *c.* 1887, photographed 1902
By kind permission of the President and Fellows of Trinity College, Oxford

The St John's College Barge

The St John's barge was built in 1891 and is unique in that it has a large and vociferous number of twentieth-century supporters, headed by Martin Slocock, an old member who bought the barge, masterminded its restoration and who conducts its after life. This support is fortuitous and compensates for the paucity of material on the early life of the barge in the St John's College archives. St John's appears at first glance to be one of the few colleges to have owned only one barge. The *Captain's Book*, dated May 30th 1854, in the Bodleian Library states that 'St John's bumped Exeter opposite the barge ...'; this could well be a rented barge but nevertheless its existence is not apparent within the St John's College archives.[152] Sherwood does mention that St John's took the Green Barge after Hall died when Salter 'became possessed of both barges (Green and Red) *c*. 1870s so it would seem that they did in fact use two barges.[153] Richard Norton believes Exeter rented both. Sherwood also writes that after 1877 St John's used the shared barge.[154]

The barge of 1891 is 70' long with eight elongated casement windows with squared upper lights. Her stern rises dramatically to form a galleon poop with tapered and angled inset sashes to her side and forward. Three rounded oeil de boeuf windows decorate the sides of this sweep. She is, perhaps, the barge with the most seamanlike feel to her, modelled, some say, with the air of an 'an eighteenth-century warship'. Her stern bears the St John's college emblem of the lamb. Her upper deck is protected by wooden railings decorated with ball finials,

A letter dated 22nd October 1922 in the college archives

The St John's College barge of 1891
Photograph by permission of St John's College, Oxford

records that it was discovered 'at the end of last term that the hull of the barge was rotten throughout and that it was necessary to build a new hull at a cost of £650'. A rebuilding fund was set up; the greater part of the college records on the barge are a copious collection of letters to this effect, from as far away as the Ministry of Finance in Cairo, including bundles of advice:[155]

> I hope the new hull will be built of sound stuff and periodically scraped and coated with a proper mixture

Another writes 'I did not have the use of the barge but I believe I contributed to the cost of its purchase and gave three guineas'.[156] The Reverend A. Ferguson wrote of the 18,000 poor in his parish and was for this reason unable to contribute and R.H. Jenkin enclosed seven shillings and six pence, 'a small offering to such a noble purpose.' R.A. Finn of Surbiton suggested that 'perhaps some of the more wealthy members of the college may stump up as well'. On a more interesting note he added 'I think you could get something out of the old gentleman who lived in Oxford and turned up for tea every day in Eights Week'. Judging by the letters it was a healthy response.

The second restoration of the St John's barge began in the 1960s (a new boathouse was built for the college in 1961). The barge was put up for sale by the college and bought by a consortium of former Boat Club members, 'a group of mid-fifties contemporaries for whom the barge was a much loved feature of every day life at Oxford'. The price paid was £115.

The St John's College barge, 1998

One of them, Mike Day, was the son of a city policeman. He remembers the barges on the towpath as a small child and particularly during his days at Magdalen College School, where the memory of a sunken barge was quite haunting to him as a young boy. He seems to remember the barge as a scene for 'romantic trysts' but is not too keen to elaborate. Peter Johnson, an old member remembers the saloon door wide open with the boiler steaming (this was often apparently out of operation).

By 1967 St John's Barge Limited was set up as a company of charitable status with its board of Oxford graduates, founder members including Richard Popplewell, Peter Treloar, Peter Johnson and Mrs Slocock. These loyal hearties scraped, cleaned and painted the forlorn old barge. Robert Maccoun was to lay his hand to the St John's barge, fitting a steel shoe under her hull, as he had done to the Corpus Christi and Hertford barges. After fitting of the hull, lack of finance proved a delay to any further works.

However, help was at hand by late 1989; Peter Johnson had a joinery business which provided elm and knot oak for the restoration at the Ailsa-Perth Shipbuilders of Troon at a cost of £25,000 (distance did not deter them). Peter Waymouth the managing director of the yard was an old friend of Martin Slocock. A subscription leaflet was printed. She was lifted (in similar fashion to the Univ barge in 1987 using the Univ's spreader beams and the same lifting company Terra Nova) with massive strops at Abingdon, having been floated downstream from Iffley and then sent by low loader up to Troon.[157] Here their draftsman executed a plan and elevation and work began.

Miraculously Ailsa Perth kept to their original estimate. Peter Johnson's woodwork company did a great deal of joinery, including replacing most of the windows and the welcoming double doors. The bench seats that line the large saloon are original, as is the decorative fireplace still standing in the barge.

The Beetle and Wedge at Wallingford provided a new home for this galleon where she was put to use for 'small conferences and entertaining'. One of the aims of the company was to 'make the barge available to a wider audience and to raise money for its maintenance by taking her to regattas and other events on the Thames'. This has to a large extent been achieved. Today, amidst good security she rests in a little backwater at the Four Pillars Hotel at Sandford, operating as an adjunct to the hotel. She is therefore, although still owned by the charitable company of old members, trading her station on a semi-commercial basis.

THE WADHAM COLLEGE BARGE

Wadham College succumbed to the lure of the barges by 1897. Wadham Boat Club records indicate that they 'took a more comfortable room at Hall in 1869 and Hall have since fitted it up with wash basins'. At this time the expenditure increased to around £80 annually. Sherwood writes that they had a room in Salter's barge; C.S.L. Davies' history of the College confirms that from 1886-97 the college hired a barge.[158] Wells' *History of Wadham College* indicates that the Boat Club's debt to Salter's had been paid off by the 1880s; this is confirmed by a letter dated March 10th 1886 in the archives.[159] The letter also states that Wadham hired a barge which 'was placed by Thames Conservancy Board in an excellent position and found to be a great convenience to the boating men'. A punt and piles for the barge were purchased. Sherwood also writes that in 1887 'Wadham took possession of … [Magdalen's] old [barge]' (there are no records to confirm this).[160] By the late 1890s the general feeling was that the college, in keeping with others, should have a barge of its own; only Lincoln and Keble were bargeless, Lincoln having permanent quarters in the OUBC boathouse. The hired barge was described as 'very ugly, badly constructed and uncomfortable', the *Wadham Gazette* described it as 'small and inconvenient'. Additionally it was let out to other parties and 'it was deemed humiliating to the college to see its colours hired out to strangers'.

The Boat Club records of Michaelmas Term 1896 wrote that 'at a general college meeting it was proposed the college should purchase a barge of its own'. An estimate for the new barge was put at an economical £550; a committee was formed and £215 was raised with £50 from the United Clubs. A letter of November 26th 1897 published in the *Wadham College Gazette* wrote that 'the college have succeeded in obtaining an excellent barge for the college Boat Club.'[161] It thanked Mr Struben, whose idea it was and who supervised the construction. The Boat Club records of 1897, written by Struben, the Captain, state that 'though failure on the river has met me with every turn I can look back with satisfaction on the fact that after two years persistence I have persuaded the college to buy a barge of its own'.[162] The barge was described as 'one of the most comfortable on the river'. Donations received totalled just over £468, a further ten shillings was raised from each freshman to achieve the figure.

There appear to be little further references to the barge. Robert Maccoun, the naval engineer made a report on her by 1973, declaring its 'vertical framing sound', but the capitals over the pilasters were in need of repair, along with the deck and planking. The hull needed a complete replacement. Maccoun recommended a steel hull at a cost of roughly £3,000, with his overall estimate being in the region of £14,000. This never materialised; the Wadham barge was sold in 1973 to a Mr Good of Hanborough who ran a window and office cleaning

The Wadham barge *c.* 1897, photographed in the 1970s
By kind permission of the Warden and Fellows of Wadham College, Oxford and Oxfordshire County Council Photographic Archive

business and had plans for a floating restaurant at a gravel pit in Cassington.[163] There is a rather forlorn picture of her on a slipway where she was lifted and 'departed on a low loader to the Cherwell as a tea house', – fate unknown.

A photograph in the archives *c.* 1897 shows the Wadham barge, built for the college by Talboys. It is a simple superstructure with trefoil windows redolent of the Arts and Crafts manner of the time.

Norman Dix remembers high jinks one night with the Wadham barge. One Rag Regatta in the 1950s the Univ men pulled a piano on a gardener's trolley down through the meadow, even stopping on the way down Broadwalk to play it. Norman would not allow the piano on the Univ barge. However the Wadham men took up the idea and decided to bring a piano down to their barge. A lot of drink was consumed and Norman had what he describes as an 'odd feeling' at home that evening and decided to go down to the Wadham barge. He found the piano overboard, the men playing overboard too, all of them plastered in mud trying to retrieve the main frame from a particular brand of Isis suction mud.

THE ST EDMUND HALL BARGE

The St Edmund Hall barge seems to fit in around this period. *The St Edmund Hall Magazine* of 1975-6 carries a small article on the barge; this records that a barge was rented from Salter's from 1898 through to 1938.[164] One old member recalls the barge being used for their pre-rowing exercises, a usage probably common to all the barges. In 1938 the college moved their headquarters to the OUBC; Norman Dix remembers them occupying a side room in the building. She was eventually purchased by an Oxonian in 1966 and endowed

The St Edmund Hall barge *c.* 1880s
By kind permission of Oxfordshire County Council Photographic Archive

with the name 'Wanderlust'; by 1972 she was converted by Salter's into a houseboat and renamed 'Ataraxia' for her new owners, A. Wheeler and C. Rayner, being resident at Harts Boat Yard, Surbiton. Three years later she was moved to London and had an outboard engine fitted, seemingly the only college barge to suffer such an indignity. The aft end became a kitchen, bathroom and workshop with living and sleeping quarters in what was originally the clubroom. In the 1980s a Young Generation dancer, Carol Forbes, lived on board and she eventually came to Thames and Kennet Marina where David Sheriff bought 'Teddars' as she was then known and carried out some restoration work, with a £20,000 budget. This including new windows with a squared window heading rather than the original plywood round heads, which proved too expensive to replace. Internal woodwork, a repaint and a smart carpet in St Edmund Hall colours were added; she was never lifted. Shiela Lovejoy, a former Reading policewomen bought her from David Sherriff and now moors the barge near Caversham Bridge at Reading. The barge was described in a 1938 issue of the Magazine as 'rapidly decaying' but the pinewood structure still held pretty sound well into the late 1990s, although she is probably nearing her time for lifting and further refurbishment.

THE KEBLE COLLEGE BARGE

Keble College, although one of the last to commission a barge, did in fact build one of the most magnificent, rumoured to vie with Pembroke in the beauty stakes. In 1899, the magnificent shape of the Keble barge, complete with Art Nouveau swirling lines to her bow and exuberant oeil de boeuf windows, emerged from the Salter's boathouse. The picture

The Keble barge photographed *c.* 1900s
By kind permission of the Warden and Fellows of Keble College, Oxford.

shown opposite is slightly out of focus; later pictures showing the barge in a more distressed state, reveal the full extent of her decorative force.

Described as 'old fashioned' in that she followed the format of previous barges, her decoration was notably modern being a mixture of Edwardian Baroque and Art Nouveau; the Art Nouveau's sinuous lines being very much in vogue at the time. She stands seemingly in complete contrast to the Gothic austerity of Butterfield's (1814-1900) college buildings that Keble occupies. In decorative terms she sported seven bell-shaped casement windows, divided by pilasters followed by four exuberantly-decorated round windows, styled as casements with top opening lights above, divided by small colonettes and spandrels with foliate decoration. The upper deck was surrounded by a turned railing, its lower section being infilled with cartouches. A further rendition of the college arms stood above the main entrance to the barge, the overhanging of the upper deck being supported by four turned columns below. Complete fantasia overcomes the barge to her stern; from the austerity of the clapperboard there emerges from the base a quartet of elongated windows, balanced by half-bell single lights to each side. Centrally the magnificent carved figure of a demonic sea satyr, bulging muscle, bearded and cloven-footed seemingly supports, with crouched body, the rounded overhang of the upper poop deck above. This is the nautical baroque performed with a vengeance. An ornately carved oval cartouche holds the Keble arms. To the sides of this are two round windows whose wave-like carving

The Art Nouveau clapper-boarded stern with balustrading and escutcheon of the Keble barge

extends to join the main cartouche. To the left is positioned a main elongated pilaster which rises the full height of the bay. This has a capital which forms a 'bat'-like play on the Ionic order and whose garland sweeps down to the windows below. Powerful and evocative, such a stern must have left a strong impression on many an Oxonian.

The *Keble College Record* of 1958 confirms that Salter Brothers supplied the college with details of the barge's construction. The hull was 'laid down and building began in May 1898, the saloon in July and the whole complete by March 1899 at a contract price of £850'. The final accounts stood at just over £936, which included such additional items as 'four galvanised buckets, washstand, lining bath and pump room, the printing and gilding of the college crest on the shield at the stern'. Gale's account for carving alone, which is particularly notable, came to £77. Sadly not a clue exists in the archives as to the architect of the barge. Good quality pitch pine was used, with a specification of 2" elm for the bottom and 1½" oak for the sides.

Few details exist in the Keble archives save that by 1958 the barge was leaking badly with extensive rot to the hull. She was pumped out frequently and blue clay 'puddled' to the inner walls of her hull in a desperate attempt to save her from a watery death. *The Record* recounts that 'the College has had to abandon the barge which has served us for the past fifty nine years!'[165] The Keble barge, undoubtedly one of the most splendid, with a virtuoso performance of carving, caught the imagination of the college cook, Mr Davey, whose gallant attempts to rescue her are recorded by the College magazine.[166] Being forbidden to sink the barge by the Thames Conservancy and with the planning authority's refusal for it to sit on dry land, the enterprising Davey, who owned a meadow near Iffley Lock, concocted a scheme to thwart the two authorities.

He dug a trench in his meadow to the dimensions of the barge, two feet deep. The river level 'was allowed to rise through an accidental delay in adjusting the flood gates and water flowed into the excavation'. *The Record* notes 'hurriedly the barge was released and propelled downstream under power of a tractor;' this whole manoevre took place in difficult winds. Len Andrew's brother, the Exeter boatman, helped. 'As in Noah's flood the waters retreated and the Keble barge rested on its Ararat'. Thames Conservancy were indignant that the bank of the river had been broken but this was quickly mended, the barge was afloat, not on land, but protected in somewhat unusual circumstances by the crafty cook.

The barge is believed to have been broken up; luckily some parts have been preserved in the Oxford City Museum, which give an inkling of her extravagant style. Notes in the Jesus College archives dated 1967 indicate that Robert Maccoun had made some estimates for restoration of the barge at approximately £11,600, but this was not taken up.

The College Record of 1958 mentioned that they purchased the 'Magdalen Barge for £500, which from an aesthetic point of view ... falls sadly short of its predecessor'. The Keble romanticists, staving off the prospect of a purpose-built boathouse, must have purchased the Magdalen College barge as the 'new barge, resplendently if curiously decorated, with heraldic emblems was brought into use for Eight's Week and members were able to view the races without fear of shipwreck'.

Opposite: the Keble barge in new found home, photographed c. 1950s
By kind permission of the Warden and Fellows of Keble College, Oxford

The Lincoln College Barge

The Lincoln barge is believed to have been built in the late nineteenth century; the college unfortunately holds no records, except for the photograph below which hangs in the Boathouse. Norman Dix recalls that Wilfred or 'Tricky' Bossom was their waterman, a 'marvellous man, born on a barge', one of the very best professional coaches who never raised his voice, never gave his rowing secrets away and always 'left something up his sleeve'. Sherwood writing in 1900 notes that Lincoln did use the Bullingdon barge, normally used as a dining club.[167] In the 1935 Summer Eights she stood down near the New Cut in between the Jesus and Trinity College barges.

A good Dixonian yarn exists about the Lincoln barge, believed to have been built in the early 1900s, which sank in 1948. It had what he called 'a peculiar pumping system', the pumps being either used to expel the bilges or pump water in. On this particular day the bilge valves were not shut, the water poured in and the barge eventually sank in nine feet of water. The Thames Conservancy came to the rescue with a pair of divers and two hefty cables around the barge. The fire brigade also rallied, no doubt at 'full pelt', and the barge rose to the surface to the cost of £50. She took a fortnight to clean out. She was used by the Oxford University College Servants Society for their rowing outings every fortnight to change on board. Norman believes she was sold to a private buyer; she was taken down to Abingdon by Len Andrews, but who bought her and where she ultimately went remains another mystery.

The Lincoln barge photographed *c.* 1904
By kind permission of Lincoln College, University of Oxford

The Hertford College Barges

Richard Norton, an old member of Hertford, is the acknowledged expert (along with Norman Dix) on the Oxford college barges. He reveals that Hertford College owned two barges, the first being built in 1877. It was only after Henry Boyd became Principal (1877-1922) Norton writes, that the Boat Club sprang to life and another barge was built in 1911[168] The college owns a photograph of the first barge,shown on page 94.

This first barge was of simple clapper board construction with seven sashes to each side and an elongated sash to the stern. Decorative features included simple attenuated pilasters with bosses and a plain railing to the upper deck. The old barge became a boat house by the Free Ferry, which Norton suggests was most likely across the New Cut on the river at Oxford.[169]

Two designs were submitted for the second Hertford barge. The architect F. W. Troup's (1859-1941) particularly extravagant design is interesting as it shows a rejected barge, unexecuted not surprisingly it is believed on the grounds of cost. Troup indulged his fantasies with the notion of an arcade of pilasters and columns headed by what appear to be classical roundels. Added to this was a particularly attractive glazed Romanesque access to the bow, round and oval windows to the stern (the latter reminiscent of Jackson's Corpus Christi barge) and a fretwork balustrading to the upper deck. It would have proved an exciting addition to the oeuvre of the Oxford college barges.

The second Hertford barge was designed in 1910 and was to cost no more than £1,000. She was first used by the college for Eights Week in May 1911. Described as 'remarkably fine' she stood three feet taller than her counterparts; this was to be to her disadvantage as she was unable to negotiate the bridges to Henley. In her tall superstructure she sported five heavily-paned rectangular windows to each side, intersected by Doric pilasters, a door being placed after the fourth window, near to the stern, with the typical bell-shaped heading of the period. Her aft end was prettily decorated with oeil de boeuf windows dressed with, what appear to be, swags and tails of a foliate nature. A sprung hood supporting Doric columns stood to the bow of the boat, which held the college arms. To her top deck encased panelling was positioned on the slightly raised stern, with railings decorated with ball finials amidships. Described as having a 'temple like structure' she was a classically-embellished barge, with a somewhat boxy appearance. An article written by the Trust for the Preservation of Oxford College Barges describes her as 'original in design' being the work of George Drinkwater (1880-1941), who they write, was a pupil of Sir Thomas Jackson (1835-1924). William Whyte writes that he is unable to substantiate this, Jackson's lists of pupils being difficult to track down, due to lack of evidence to date. Drinkwater's name is apparently not on the original drawing of the barge.

The *Hertford College Magazine* of 1911 cites 'The habitual critics who were silent when suggestions were wanted for the design of a new Barge, have just spent a very enjoyable month in voicing all sorts of ingenious objections to the Barge as it now appears'. Later in the year she apparently 'won general admiration', although the critics disparaged the 'stunted appearance of its prow and the discomfort of its perpendicular staircase'; both faults were apparently remedied

Her story however is a sad one. Highlighted as the Trust's flagship for restoration in 1967 (having been donated in 1966) she was unfortunately burnt out by vandals on May 19th 1969, the whole of her superstructure being destroyed.[170]. Maccoun had previously set to work on the barge; he found a secondhand cargo barge in the Pool of London, built in 1924. This was adapted and repaired at a cost of £800, as opposed to £2,500 for a 'new steel job'. He somewhat ingeniously used two old narrow boats (in a makeshift dry dock in the New Cut) to sandwich the

The first Hertford barge – Summer Eights *c.* 1908
With permission from the Principal, Fellows and Scholars of Hertford College in the University of Oxford

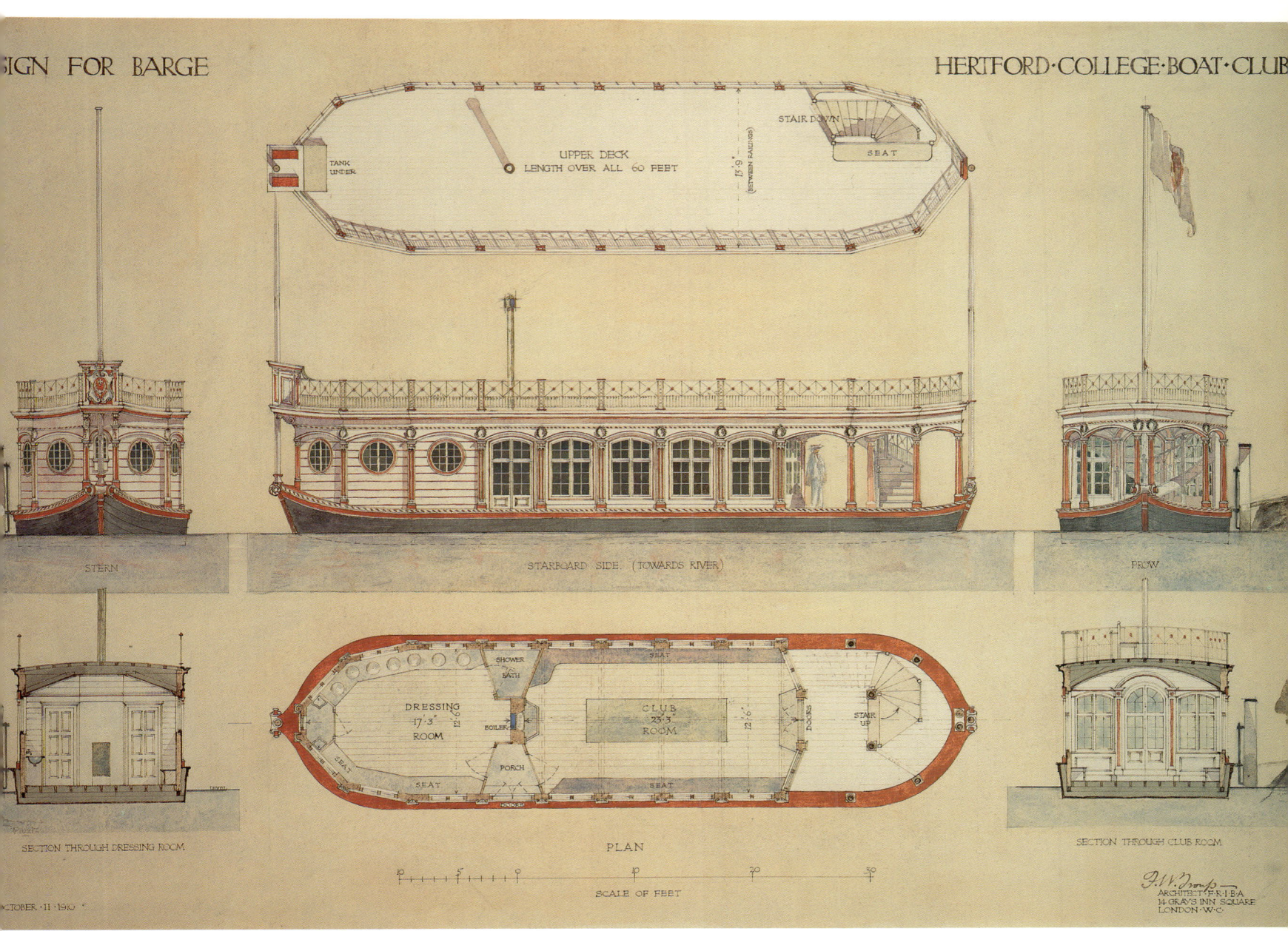

Rejected design for barge – F. W. Troup 1910
With permission from the Principal, Fellows and Scholars of Hertford College in the University of Oxford

hull of the Hertford barge and then act as an hydraulic lift.[171] He filled their holds with water and then emptied them, leaving the hull suspended so that he was able to 'saw off the old hull and let it down on its new one'. Insurance claims after the fire enabled the Trust to send the barge up to Tough Brothers of Teddington for a rebuild of her superstructure. Even then she was still too tall to pass through all the bridges and had to be ballasted down with fifty-five tons of water and the railings removed. Norman Dix tells a story of a panic telephone call asking his advice; apparently the barge, on its journey home was stuck under Cliveden Bridge. either they had taken some of the ballast out or the water level was higher than normal. The only solution was to lower the water levels in the reach.

Sadly the Preservation Trust's flagship, with Phoenix overtones, was hit again by vandals on July 7th 1997; she went up in flames, the sole remains being a burnt and rusty old hull at Sandford. Fresh news from Richard Norton relates that Orde Levinson, an old Magdalen member, has purchased the hull with plans to rebuild the Hertford barge and use her as an annex to a proposed restaurant at Oxford.

The second Hertford College barge – Summer Eights 1911
With permission from the Principal, Fellows and Scholars of Hertford College in the University of Oxford

The Merton College Barges

Although at one point it appeared that no one remembered a Merton barge, Rodney Needham, writing from All Souls College, put the record straight. He certainly recalls the Merton barge, not long after World War II. It is a romantic recollection, of 'dappled light flickering on the ceiling of the main chamber'; he writes that he had never seen such an effect in any other setting – 'it was enchanting'. Sherwood notes that Merton used the shared barge around 1900, so it would appear that the Merton barge was probably of early twentieth-century origin. However Dr Michael Stansfield, while archivist of Merton, recently brought to light a ledger of Boat Club accounts dating from 1860 which provide irrefutable proof that Merton had use of a barge from that time and similarly has produced a picture of the Merton barge c. 1903.

The leather bound accounts book entitled *Merton Boat Club* shows income and expenditure for the period 1860 to 1882. The first entry bearing possible reference to a barge is 'Randall's bill for Flag – £1.4s'; it is possible that this could refer to a flag for use on the OUBC barge. On June 18th 1860 a payment was made to the boatman Mr Hall for £12.8.0d; this could have been rental fee for a barge, other college's boat club accounts show similar amounts. An entry dated May 3rd 1863 provides conclusive proof of a Merton barge; 18/6d was paid out for 'basons, [and] jug for dressing room'; the aft end of the college barges provided changing rooms for the rowers. On June 5th 1864 the boatman Tims was paid 'for bringing water to the barge', a duty he was to perform regularly during the period of the ledger. In March 1866 the boatbuilders Salter's submitted an account for £67.6.6d, an enormous amount in boat club terms of the period; although unspecified it would seem likely this was for restoration works to the barge, or even for the commissioning of a new one. In November 1873 a Mr Evans was paid for a settee and tablecloth, Tims continued to supply the barge periodically with water and Slatter and Rose provided the mental sustenance of papers and periodicals, as they did to other college barges. In October 1877 a bookshelf was put into the barge; further minutiae included 'shoehorns for the barge' in 1879 and buttonhooks in 1880. In the early 1880s a mackintosh and rug were purchased and later in the decade three armchairs, new curtains and a new supply of towels further added to the comfort of the vessel. The Boat Club accounts therefore provide definitive proof of an early Merton barge. Robert Hill's linen-bound photo album, embroidered with the initials 'M.C.' additionally provides further evidence of the early twentieth-century barge.

This is a clapper-boarded vessel showing six plain elongated casements to each elevation with a side entrance of six lights positioned after the first window. The aft end is more decorative, showing a rounded sweep with four casements divided by pilasters with collared bosses. The upper deck is finished with plain railings, which are decorated only to the stern with ornate flourishes. The major portion of the upper deck is covered in a striped awning; the outer staircase, flagpole and college arms are standard to the barges generally. Some creature comforts are evident in the photograph: generous velvet cushions soften the prow creating further seating and a samovar-like tea urn provides refreshment to the Merton supporters on the upper deck.

Dr Roger Highfield of Merton College suggested the letters of K. Zachariah, an undergraduate at Merton, whose diary dating from 1912-15 could throw some light on the subject of the barge. Zachariah's account of his journey to Oxford starts from the *S.S. Bengala* sailing from India through the Red Sea and up the Suez Canal. On reaching London he stayed at the Indian National Association in Cromwell Road and hence to Oxford, where the 'buildings all tower and battlement and hoary looking, homes of ancient learning,' deeply impressed the young man.[172]

Increasingly worried by the cold, lack of funding and the problem of finding a college willing to admit him, he eventually is offered a place at Merton, where there is one other Indian, who is 'exceedingly querulous'. His diaries make anecdotal and pithy social observations. They range from observing the 'ugly habit of raining ... it drizzles enough to annoy you' ... to varsity fashions of the period. Zachariah commented on the 'broad brogue shoes, gorgeous cloxed [chequered] stockings, wide rather than narrow trousers, low waistcoats, quite round edged coats, very low collars if stiff, if soft, (more in vogue) taffeta Shakespeare style, pinned together below the knot'.[173] He shows interest in the Boat Club but recounts 'the boat does not want me and I cannot risk my life playing rugby and soccer', but nevertheless determines 'to do walking and sculling on the upper river'. An entry for October 1912 recounts him walking the lower river where all the college barges were moored. Zachariah noted that 'one of the boats was tied immovably to the barge' (an early form of rowing tank). Apparently the Captain stood by the side handing out instructions to the fresher who had to row, 'never of course making any progress and this for half an hour, jolly hard work I say'.

Zachariah also writes of 'running along the tow path cheering the Merton Eight', 'all shorts and stockings with pistols and trumpets, bells and rattles'. He was unsure of the spelling: whether it be 'toepath' or towpath, deciding eventually 'it might be either because it is only three or four foot wide'. In November Zachariah 'took a light boat and rowed up to the mill'; rowing was gradually becoming a part of his undergraduate life. He notes with the perspicacity of a foreigner the Oxford tendency of the time to add the suffix 'er' to words; the Radcliffe Library was known as 'Radders', breakfast 'brekker,' the Torpid races 'Toggers' and the Prince of Wales up at Oxford at the time and a subject of some fascination to Zachariah, 'Pragger Wagger'. Further words to be learnt were 'slime' for treacle, 'squish' for marmalade and 'sand' for sugar.[174]

May 1913 was Zachariah's first Eights Week. He recalls 'the monotonous dark of mens' and womens' clothes of winter have given place to colours, which in some ladies' dresses are nearly outrageous'. The tops of the barges were covered with awnings and below were the visitors. Merton, making 'one tremendous spurt' bumped Balliol, the cheering was stupendous, the crew all 'jumped into the river and swam across to the barge'; this was Zachariah's first mention of the Merton barge itself.[175]

Eights Week of 1914 is similarly described: 'there were scores of punts and scores of ladies in them and on the barges ... dirty children paddled on the river banks, eightsmen strutted up and down in all the glory of coloured blazers, the man who caught the crab [for Merton – Balliol bumped them] refused to be comforted and wept like Rachael'.[176]

As for the war, by 1915 'Oxford pursues its usual course, undeterred by the blockade and Zeppelins which might drive us into the cellars, still the dons lecture'. His eventual departure from England in November 1915 was 'a most tearful business'; he took up a post at the Presidency College of Calcutta. His diaries are a fascinating account of undergraduate life of the period; they are particularly interesting in that the perspective is non-European and refreshingly honest.

A photograph album presented to the college in December 1976 by Sir Basil Blackwell (Merton 1907–11), features a small and somewhat unfocused picture of the interior of the barge.

Dr Highfield believes that the barge would most likely have had the college shield on its stern, with the arms of Walter de Merton, its founder; this is confirmed by the 1903 photograph. It is believed to have been turned into a house boat and moored in a cut between Oxford and Iffley, on the Iffley side of the river. The last mention falls to Len Andrews, brother of the Exeter boatman, who remembers that in the 1940s Salter's bought the Merton barge and Hubert Salter lived on it, until she was eventually broken up.

The Merton College barge *c.* 1903
By kind permission of The Warden and Fellows of Merton College Oxford.
Robert Hill's photograph album McPh/A1/4

Other Barges

The Bullingdon Club barge *c.* 1890s
By kind permission of the Master and Fellows of University College, Oxford

St Peter's, St Anne's and St Hugh's did not, according to their archivists, have a barge. St Peter's is mentioned on the plan of the barges featured in the Summer Eights of 1935, they probably occupied the Green Barge. The St Catherine's barge – the old Balliol barge – stood at the head above Merton in the same year.[177] Norman Dix remembers the waterman on the Green Barge; if any student were caught using foul language the 'Bibleman' would get out his book and refer the offender to the relevant text. Salter's barges were apparently always painted green. Richard Norton owns a letter from Henry Boyd, dated 9th May 1850, describing Bumps Week, alluding to King's barge, another boatbuilder's barge owned by King and Hall, which was sometimes let out to the Bullingdon Club and others:

> at King's barge all the colours of the different boats were flying, one above the other in their order; the banks on both sides were thronged with eager spectators, the bands were playing on top of the University barge …

The Talboys barge was mentioned in the Oriel Boat Club's *Captain's Book* of 1909.[178] Other known barges include the Bullingdon barge which, as previously noted, was used as a dining room during Eights Week; for the rest of the year Salter's used it as a store room for cushions; this later became known as Loder's and Harvey's barge.[179] The OUBC ledgers of 1839-75 mention the Loder barge. Other sources mention the British Queen, and the Nelson.[180] The Victory, another barge, boasted a monumental stern articulated by two rows of nine individual sashes, divided by an arrangement of inset balusters. Richard Norton suggests the possibility that this *may* have belonged to the Queen's barge of 1872, which was large.

The Green Barge *c.* 1954
Courtesy of Norman Dix

Transported Meanings

One particularly interesting feature to emerge from study of the history of the barges is the transference of inheritance from their livery company origins to university usage. It is possible that those who instigated their purchase were fully aware of this.

The livery companies as ancient trade fellowships, similar to the northern guilds, are medieval foundations and therefore share Oxford's medieval origins. Both were reliant on a form of private membership and publicly held in high esteem. Both were wealthy, sporting grand buildings with ornate trappings. The livery companies' love of pageantry would probably have appealed to the nineteenth-century Oxonian. Each livery company had a symbol, emblazoned on arms signifying their origins to the outside world. The Oxford colleges followed this tradition; the college arms and symbols were comfortable replacements.

The early barges adapted usage can be said to be particularly inspired, the product of innovative thinking, primarily provoked by the development of rowing at Oxford. The Oxford college barges were undoubtably a one-off concept; nothing is really comparable in boating terms. The barges helped to foster undivided collegiate loyalty by their individual iconography. Each of the colleges in this history was able to establish its individual mark on the river at Oxford and carry the college identity away from the solidity of stone or brick to something more theatrical. College colours, flags and arms, supported by the camaraderie developed within the barges, was to make them spirit raisers and rallying points during the races; a loud cheer from the college barge when rowing past undoubtedly inspired the oarsmen's strength and determination. They were used as sports rooms, clubhouses, common rooms, storage places for boating equipment, meeting places for romantic trysts, party locations and undoubtedly escapist bolt holes from the rigours of academic life. The memorial barges of Corpus Christi and the second Magdalen barge are particularly evocative. Interior photographs are particularly rare, four are shown on following pages.

One interior shot is credited as the Queen's barge *c*. 1898. It features the central table, writing materials, fireplace and shows the leisured ambience on board.

The OUBC barge was, until the boathouse was built, the official 'office' of the Club; all club notices and edicts were issued from its timbered frame. It was also used as a reading room and 'was the only reading-room open on Sundays in those day ... hence it was no reflection on the OUBC if a man of shady social status joined the UBC Barge'.[181] Woodgate declared some of the men not 'sound' and because of this formed a dining club called Vincents which is still in existence today.

In artistic terms the barges represent the varying movements or 'battle of the styles': the Gothic OUBC, the classical Hertford, the Art Nouveau of Keble and the Edwardian Baroque of Pembroke. The use of the column with its accompanying orders is a recurring feature. This is notable on the Jesus barge with its Ionic capitals, and the now extinct Hertford's Doric columns. The orders derived from the buildings of ancient Greece and Rome carried varying meanings; the Doric order spoke of manliness, strength and virility, the Ionic was considered a more feminine order redolent of wisdom and the Corinthian a more matronly order associated with luxury. These combined with sweeping sterns, elegant figureheads, varied window configurations, elaborate balconies and varnished 'clubby interiors' collectively created a unique genre. The Magdalen barge was one of the most decorated with college symbols. Railings to their upper decks

The Interior of the Univ barge *c.* 1952
Courtesy of Norman Dix

and often a figurehead to their bow alongside the ubiquitous college crest were means employed to display the college iconography. The Pembroke barge (1903) showed the rose on its railings, the second Corpus barge of the same year displayed what appeared to be the Maude family crest and possibly some college symbol (this is not clear from the photographs). The Trinity barge of 1887 shows a cross/lozenge type decoration to the stern and the Christ Church barge a star-like symbol.

The patronage of architects is an important element of the barges' history and probably one that is not generally known to architectural historians. The commissions ranged from the homely Drinkwater to the more eminent T. G. Jackson and John Oldrid Scott. The barges must have been an inspiring divertissement for the architects employed, demanding an

The interior of the Magdalen barge *c.* 1928
By kind permission of the President and Fellows of Magdalen College, Oxford

alternative and rather quirky skill from their offices. Some 'architectless' barges manage, probably with the skill of Salter's the boatbuilders, to muster a degree of difference; even the most plain supercede the derogatory label of 'huts on rafts'.

However evocative, lovable or grand, the death knell of the barges had been sounded by the early 1920s; a letter in the OUBC archive states that three colleges were hoping to acquire sites for boathouses as they could no longer afford the expense of the barges'.[182] A much later article in the *London Illustrated News* of 1956, interviewing the President of the OUBC suggests that the disappearance of the barges at Oxford was a 'sign of the fact that there was no longer a leisured class at Oxford'. The sport of rowing had escalated in popularity, larger premises were needed, costs needed to be

The interior of the Christ Church barge *c.* 1902
The National Monuments Record Office

cut, modernism with its inherent functionalism was in favour.

Some old diehards clung to the tradition of the barges; the Trust for their preservation highlighted their plight. It is an extraordinary fact that in 2003 ten barges are still in existence of an original estimated twenty-five, their usage varying still from clubhouse to pleasure palace.

Robert Maccoun called them 'floating pavilions' but added somewhat dryly that 'they were after all beautiful, rather impractical changing rooms for oarsmen', not forgetting the boatmen who worked their lives on board.

Left: the interior of the Queen's College barge *c.* 1898
Oxfordshire County Council Photographic Archives
This page: Norman and the Angels
Courtesy of Norman Dix

Chronological Table

1839	The first barge is rented from Heather for the OUBC
1846	The OUBC purchase the Merchant Taylors' barge
1846	The Brasenose barge is first mentioned, which was used until 1857 – this may well have been the OUBC barge
1848-50	Oriel purchase the Goldsmiths' barge
1854	The OUBC commission E.G. Bruton to design their barge
1854	University College purchased the Merchant Taylors' barge
1854	First mention of a St John's College barge, probably rented
1850-56	Exeter use the Stationers' barge during this period
1857	Queen's College buy the old City or Lord Mayor's barge
1857	The first mention of a Christ Church barge
1859	Balliol purchase the Skinners' barge
1863	The first mention of a Queen's barge
1866	Trinity rents a barge from Salter's
1870	The first mention of a Pembroke barge
1871	The first mention of a Worcester barge
1872	Magdalen College hired a barge from Salter's
1872	Queen's College build a new barge
1873	It is believed Univ took the Red barge, the Stationers' city barge
1873	Salter's build the first Exeter barge
1876	Brasenose commissioned a barge
1877	First Hertford College barge built
1878	John Oldrid Scott designs the Univ barge
1879	New College commission a barge
1880	During the 1880s New College shared a barge with Pembroke, St John's and Jesus
1881	The new Balliol barge is built
1882	The new Brasenose College barge is built
1883	The Corpus Christi barge is built, having been designed by T.G. Jackson – it is believed that they had previously used the Merchant Taylors' barge
1885	It is believed the Skinners' barge was bought by Queen's from Balliol
1886	P.E. Warren prepares designs for the Magdalen College barge
1887	Jesus College commission T.G. Tagg & Sons to build a barge
1886	Wadham hired a barge from this date until 1897
1888	Trinity build a barge having previously rented from Salter's
1891	The St John's College barge is built

CHRONOLOGICAL TABLE

1892	T.G. Jackson designs the Oriel College barge
1897	Wadham College build a barge having previously rented from Hall and Salter's
1898	St Edmund Hall rent a barge from Salter's
1899	The Keble barge is built. The Lincoln barge is also believed to have been built in the late 1890s.
1900	Merton using the shared barge. Merton College built their own barge sometime in the 1900s.
1903	Pembroke build their new barge
1908	A new Queen's College barge is commissioned and built
1910	Hertford College commission their second barge from Drinkwater
1911	J.H. England prepares plans for the Jesus College barge, built by Salter's
1925	Brasenose commission their last barge
1926	The second New College barge is built, designed by George Drinkwater
1927	George Drinkwater also designs the new Magdalen College barge
1930	The second Corpus Christi barge is built designed by N.W. Harrison

Sources

Balliol College Archives
Beerbohm, M. (1911) *Zuleika Dobson*, London.
Bodleian Library, OUBC *Captain's Books* 1855-70, 1870-1880.
Brasenose College Archives
Corpus Christi College Archives.
Country Life, January 5th 1967 & November 9th 1972.
Day, M. 1991, *Journal of the Oxford Society*, vol. XL111, no.2 & correspondence.
Dix, Norman – correspondence.
Exeter College Archives.
Green, V.H. (1974) *A History of Oxford University*, London.
Harrison, B. (1994) *History of the University of Oxford*, Oxford.
Hutchins, R. (1993) *Well Rowed Magdalen*, Oxford.
Jackson. T.G. (1892) *Jackson's Recollections*, Oxford.
Jesus College Archives.
Keble College Archives.
Magdalen College Archives.
Mouchel International Archives.
Merton College Archives.
New College Archives.
Nicholls Palmer, K. (1997) *Ceremonial Barges on the River Thames*, London.
Norton, R. – correspondence.
Oriel College Archives
OUBC Archives.
Petrides, A. (1959) *State Barges on the Thames*, London.
Rivington, R.T. (1983) *Punting*, Oxford.
Royal Academy of Arts, London.
Rowntree, D. *The Architectural Review*, July 1956.

Sayle, T. (1932) *The Barges of the Merchant Taylors' Company*, London.
Stone, L. (1975) *The University in Society*, London.
St John's College Archives.
Sherwood, The Reverend W.E. (1900) *Oxford Rowing*, Oxford.
Tuckwell, W. The Reverend. (1900) *Reminiscences of Oxford*, Oxford.
Trinity College Archives.
The Oxford County Newspapers.
The Oxford Mail, May 19th 1969 & 29th May 1975.
The Oxford Magazine, vol. 1V, no.1. 27th January 1886.
The Oxford Times, May 13th 1985.
The Sunday Times, 15th May 1932.
The Trust for the Preservation of Oxford College Barges.
University College Archives.
Wadham College Archives.
Wells. H.G. (1911, 1994 edition) *The New Machiavelli*, London and USA.
William Whyte, Wadham College, Oxford – correspondence.
Woodgate, W.B. (1909) *Reminiscences of An Old Sportsman*, London.

Footnotes

[1] Richard Norton, the leading authority on the Oxford college barges, writes that they were referred to as 'Barge Men'. 'In terms of rowing barges 'Bargemasters' are something else, they take responsibility for the security of the whole crew and passengers, the coaching of the crew being a separate issue'. The term is used here in deference to the Barge Men.

[2] M.R. Day, (St John's 1955), writing in the *Journal of the Oxford Society* in 1991 believes there were a maximum of twenty-six in 1930, which by 1955 had declined to twenty-two. A drawing by Stella Newton based on the Summer Eights programme of 1935 was published in *Well Rowed Magdalen*. It shows 25 barges. The Trust for the Preservation of Oxford College Barges, founded in 1966, states in a published leaflet that there were certainly more than twenty.

[3] The remaining barges are Univ, Teddars, St John's, Magdalen, New College, Corpus, Balliol, Brasenose, Queen's and Jesus.

[4] Beerbohm, M. (1911) p. 74.

[5] Ibid. p. 75.

[6] Wells, H.G. (1911, 1994 edition). p. 307.

[7] Norton writes they visited the principal castles, palaces and sites of church and state from the Tower of London up to Windsor and down to Rochester. This would include law courts, prisons, places of execution, Parliament, Lambeth Palace, Runnymede and Somerset House.

[8] Norton adds that this order of precedence was established by the foundation date of the company.

[9] Petrides, A. (1959) p. 10.

[10] Sayle, T. (1932) p. 3.

[11] Petrides, Op.cit. This is an excerpt from Anne Boleyn's coronation procession from Greenwich to Westminster, 1533.

[12] Norton adds that the Bargemaster had a bow man to take charge of the crew and assist in manoeuvres.

[13] Sayle, T. Op. cit. p. 4.

[14] The second barge of the Merchants Taylors' Company *c.* 1717.

[15] Norton adds that 'this was in the same year that the City Barge made the voyage to Oxford and back surveying the locks and weirs'.

[16] Richard Norton notes there is a boat of 1829 in the Science Museum.

[17] Sherwood, The Rev. W. E. (1900). Norton writes that there are pictures of this in the Christ Church boathouse.

[18] Tuckwell, W. (1900).

[19] Bodleian Library Department C. 784.

[20] The first race was run in 1840 'with bachelors who had rowed in the college races'. Bodleian Library, C. 784.

[21] Bodleian Library ref: C. 784:1.

[22] Sherwood, Op. cit. p. 92. writes that in 1839 there were no college barges, but definitely King and probably Hall the boatbuilder had barges.

[23] Ibid. Heather, according to Sherwood, kept the lock at Folly Bridge. Norton believes there was a lock at Folly Bridge until 1885.

[24] One Henry Grant is paid £6 in wages in the 1840s. Hall, King, and Goatley all rendered accounts to the OUBC in 1848.

[25] Bodleian Library, C. 784 1.

[26] *OUBC Accounts Ledger* 1839-75.

[27] Norton writes this was probably 'Commem. Week, the 9th Week in summer'.

[28] Norton suggests that Queen's may well have used this barge, with its distinctive round-headed windows, after the OUBC.

[29] Bruton was the Oxford City Surveyor.

[30] Bossom's business was and still is at Binsey.

[31] Norton writes that John Clasper built boats at Long Bridges too.

[32] *Ledger Accounts OUBC*, October 1st 1876-1893. The entry does not indicate the location of Tims' new business; he was apparently, according to Norton later, at Long Bridges.

33 Notice in the notices book (*OUBC Miscellanaeous* 1878-1889) issued from the club barge, dated December 1880, states that for the trial Eights Race, which was to take place over the Moulsford course on Saturday 11 December at 3 o'clock 'a special train [will] leave Moulsford for Oxford at 4.30 for those who wish to see the race'.
34 The boathouse was burnt down the following year by suffragettes. (Zachariah, K. Oxford undergraduate correspondence, p. 125, June 4th 1913 –) (By kind permission of The Warden and Fellows of Merton College, Oxford).
35 Stone, L. (1975) p. 60.
36 Ibid. p. 67.
37 Ibid. p. 66.
38 Ibid. p. 65.
39 Green, V.H. (1974) p. 180.
40 Ibid. p. 181.
41 Ibid.
42 Ibid. p. 185.
43 Ibid. p. 180.
44 Ibid.
45 Ibid. p. 188. In October 1914 there were 1,400 graduates, which reduced to 369 in 1918.
46 Ibid. p. 189.
47 Harrison, B. (1994) p. 81.
48 Ibid. p. 91.
49 Ibid. p. 92.
50 Ibid. p. 98.
51 Ibid. p. 94.
52 Ibid p. 103.
53 Green, Op.cit. p. 193.
54 Ibid. p. 196.
55 Mike Day, letter – December 22nd 1997.
56 *See* footnote 34.
57 Rivington, R.T. (1933) p. 131.
58 Nicholls Palmer, K. (1997). This includes an appendix on the Oxford College Barges by Richard Norton, then Chairman of the Trust for the Preservation of Oxford College Barges.
59 Norton's notes in the Corpus Christi College archives show that in 1846 the Goldsmiths' barge came to Oriel College; Norton writes he believes this, but 'cannot find a definite connection'. M.R. Day writing in *The Journal of the Oxford Society* Volume XL111, no. 2 Dec 1991, states that 'several barges visited Oxford *c.* 1850'.
60 Oriel College Archives C. 1.30. This states that Varley believed there to be no foundation that the first Oriel barge was the Lord Mayor's Barge, which was a 'larger and more ornate craft'. Richard Norton is 'confident' that the Lord Mayor's Barge went to Queen's.
61 Tims, (1867).
62 Oriel College Archives C.C. 1.30, dated 19.12.1932.
63 The original Merchant Taylors' Barge length was documented as 78', with a beam of 14', built as previously described by Richard Roberts of Lambeth.
64 Nicholls Palmer, Op. cit. p. 38.
65 Sherwood, Op. cit. p. 93.
66 Sir Thomas Graham Jackson Bt RA (1835-1924) architect of the Examination Schools Oxford, 1876-82 and New Buildings, Brasenose College, 1909-11, among many other Oxford buildings.
67 Jackson, T.G. (1892) p. 233.
68 Oriel College Archives, *Captain's Record* 1892-1906, C:1:30
69 I am most grateful to William Whyte of Wadham College, Oxford for drawing my attention to these.
70 Oriel College Archives, *Captain's Record* 1913-14.
71 Oriel College Archives Oriel Boat Club, *Captain's Records* 1936-79.
72 Sherwood, W. Op cit p. 93. Norton's list in the Corpus Christi College archives gives the date 1846.
73 Bodleian Library Dept C. 785 *Captain's Books* 1855-1870, p. 141.
74 Nicholls Palmer writes that the plans for the 1800 barge, which went first to the OUBC and eventually to Univ, exist in the Merchant Taylors' Company archives.
75 University College Archives (UCA) *University College Boat Club,* vol. 1, 1892-1909. UC:04/A1/2.
76 UCA. *University College Record,* vol. V, September 1967, no 2. This is confirmed by Sherwood, W. Op cit p. 93. Norton's note in the Corpus Christi College archives indicate University College held the Stationers' barge until 1877.
77 UCA, *University College Record,* 1923-1933, p. 7.
78 UCA, *University College Boat Club,* vol. 1V, 1926-1933.
79 UCA, *The University College Record,* vol.v, September 1967, no. 2.
80 Ibid.
81 This is a section of the poem.
82 This is not proven. The Young Rower was a 'new' image of the time; that of 'the athletic river girl' and not in the words of the artist, 'the sloping shouldered type of sixty or seventy years ago'. The painting was not a portrait; the artist used a professional model, a Miss Freda Walker, according to Rochdale Art Gallery. A review in the *Sunday Times* of 15th May 1932 notes 'it is a work to which we return again and again with joy', much as has many a Univ rower. A more unusual artefact in the form of a dinosaur's bone always hung in the barge according to Norman, who

recounts this was at one time stolen, but a new one was presented by Professor Elwyn Simons.
83 Nicholls Palmer, Op. cit. p. 150. Nicholls Palmer writes that the Stationers' barge 'was bought by Mr Hall … who hired it to Exeter College in 1849 …'.
84 Norton adds that 'this fits with Salter's penchant for green barges' (Salter eventually took over King's business).
85 Sherwood, Op. cit. p. 92 & *Balliol Boat Club Journal* no. 2, Hilary Term 1859 states 'the barge was purchased from the Skinners' Company'. A photo exists of this barge in the Oxfordshire archives.
86 Norton writes that the fetching of jackets may 'refer to pea jackets which were hired out by Hall at this period'.
87 Sherwood, Op. cit. p. 28. Sherwood mentions the visit in 1863.
88 See Diana Rowntree's article 'Oxford College Barges' *The Architectural Review*, July 1956.
89 Balliol College Archives (B.C.A.) *Balliol Boat Club Journal* 1871-1885.
90 Backhouse had rowed in 1904, 1906 and 1907.
91 BCA Letter *Balliol Boat Club Records*, Richard Smith, May 1925.
92 BCA *Balliol College Boat Club Records*, 1902-27.
93 BCA *Balliol College Boat Club Records*, 1938-47.
94 Richard Norton suggests the term Bargee 'does not reflect good boat club spirit'; it is recounted in this context as original to the records and I believe refers to a student in charge of organising the barge.
95 D. Kingston, Letter 1st April 1988. Kingston remembers the barge as being 'Edwardian rather than Victorian'.
96 Norman recounts that Talboys had a licensed ferry, which 'had a wonderful line but ghastly colours; it 'disappeared downstream'. Norton writes that Tate is the landlord of downstream moorings.
97 Dr John Jones, Balliol College, letter dated 28.8.97.
98 The Queen's College archivist, J.M. Kaye writes that the barge in fact belonged to the Boat Club (letter, 2nd September 1997).
99 Sherwood, Op. cit. p. 85 & p. 94.
100 Bodleian Library, Dept. C. 785, *Captain's Book* 1855-1870. Norton's notes in the Corpus Christi College archives indicate Queen's College had this barge probably from 1857-1860.
101 Nicholls Palmer, K. Op.cit. p. 165.
102 Norton's notes in the Corpus Christi College archives indicate Queen's College owned the Skinners' barge until 1897. The 1872 barge presumably must have deteriorated by then. Nicholls Palmer indicates that the Skinners' barge 'was sold in 1858 to Mr Searle and used by Queen's College …' (Op. cit. p. 42).
103 Len Andrews, whose brother was the Exeter boatman recalls that the Queen's barge was at one time bought by a man called Leicester who owned a taxi service. He apparently put 3' of concrete into the bottom.
104 Sherwood, Op. cit. p. 93. Norton's notes in the Corpus Christi College archives indicate the OUBC barge went to Brasenose from 1846-56.
105 Brasenose College Archives (BCA) *Brasenose College Boat Club Minutes Book* 1837-72 – SL 8 B1/1.
106 BCA, *Brasenose Boat Club Records XIV I*, Diary, p. 41.
107 Woodgate, W.B. (1909) p. 185.
108 BCA, *Brasenose College Boat Club*, SL8 B1/1.
109 BCA, *Brasenose Boat Club Records*, SL8 B5.2/2.
110 BCA, *Brasenose Boat Club Records*, SL8/B5/2/3/1bb.
111 OUBC *Captains Book*, 1855-1870, Bodleian Library, Department C. 785.
112 Letter dated 8th November 1999, taken from *Boat Club Log Book*.
113 OUBC *Captain's Book* 1855-1870, p. 170.
114 Richard Norton notes that this was Clasper of Long Bridges.
115 Len Andrews too recalls her as a 'very pretty barge, painted in pinks and creams'.
116 Hutchins, R. (1993), p. 10. The map is redrawn from the *OUBC Eights Programme* of 1935 by Stella Newton.
117 Sherwood, Op. cit. p. 93. In 1901 this was still used by Merton.
118 New College Archives – second barge file.
119 Drinkwater was also later to design the second Hertford barge in 1911.
120 Letter, 1926.
121 *Country Life*, November 9th 1972.
122 Corpus Christi College Archives (CCC Archives) *The Pelican*, vol. VII, 1903-5.
123 Richard Norton is however confident that they were used by Corpus Christi.
124 William Whyte writes that Jack Lanchester's Catalogue of Jackson's Oxford work records that he designed a barge for Corpus.
125 William Whyte, Wadham College, Oxford, letter 17.2.1998.
126 *Oxford Magazine*, vol. IV, no. 1, 27th January 1886.
127 The second Corpus barge was the last of the Oxford college barges to be built.
128 CCC Archives. *The Pelican Record*, vol. XIX, no. 6th June 1930.
129 Harrison is not listed in *Who's Who in Architecture*.
130 The pelican was part of the personal seal of the college founder, Bishop Fox of Winchester.
131 CCC Archives, ADD/971/6.
132 *The Pelican Record*, Op.cit.
133 The Trust for the Preservation of Oxford College Barges Appeal lists Sir Hugh Casson as one of the Trustees, Aubrey Boweden, Timothy Cornish, Peter Edwards, Michael Gee and Sarah Hosking as Founders, with a venerable list of sponsors, including John Betjeman, Osbert

Lancaster, and Sir John Summerson amongst others. It had an 'executive committee of nine' including Lady Wheare.

134 Richard Norton writes that the Trust for the Preservation of the Oxford College Barges is now run by George Marshall and is concentrating on refurbishing the Corpus barge. (letter 8th December 2000).
135 Sherwood, Op. cit. p. 93.
136 Jesus College Archives (JCA) Jesus College Barge Committee February 1887.
137 Richard Norton notes that this was a company which had itself been the owner of a barge.
138 JCA, *Jesus College Boat Club* – SO.2.1V.
139 JCA, *Jesus College Boat Club Accounts*, 1889-1900 – SO.2.V.
140 JCA, *Jesus College Boat Club*, Archives 65/68 issue 2.
141 *Oxford Today*, Trinity 1990, vol. 2. no. 3. An article was also written on the Jesus college barge in *Country Life* 1967.
142 Magdalen College Archives (MCA) *Magdalen College Boat Club Records*, Scrap Book – W.D. McCray, 11838-1891, 827 (ii).
143 Hutchins, R. (1993) p. 20 & Sherwood, Op. cit. p. 89. Norman Dix recounts that the Green Barge was later in this century owned by Salter's and used as a changing room for St Peter's and St Catherine's.
144 OUBC Records, *Captain's Book*, 1870-1880.
145 Sherwood, Op. cit. p. 89.
146 MCA, *Magdalen College Boat Club Records*, (MS 1014) 19.12.33.
147 Sherwood, Op. cit. p. 95.
148 MCA, Magdalen College Boat Club 1907-1926, *Oxford College Barge Potted History*, MS958, October 1907.
149 Mouchel International Archives, *Ferro-Concrete Barge at Oxford*, 1927, p. 259.
150 Trinity College Archives, (TCA) *Trinity College Boat Club*, Archives B/BC/3.2.
151 Trinity College Archivist, Mrs C.J. Hopkins, letter September 11th, 1997.
152 Bodleian Library, *Captain's Books* 1855-70, C. 785.
153 Sherwood, Op. cit. p. 93. Norton's list lodged in the Corpus Christi archives dates this barge as being owned by St John's from 1973-91.
154 Ibid.
155 St John's College Archives (SJCA) *St John's College*, no. 270, box file 9.
156 Ibid. ref. Archibald Allen.

157 *The Oxford Times*, May 13th, 1985.
158 Davies, C.S.L. (1994) p. 48. & Sherwood, Op. cit. p. 89.
159 J.B. Wells, (1898) & Wadham College Archives (WCA) ref. 11.5 *Miscellaneous Collection*. A further letter dated December 14th 1896 mentions the old members' kindness in paying off the debt to Salter's.
160 Sherwood, Op. cit. p. 95.
161 WCA, *Wadham College Gazette*, vol. 1, no. 1, 1897.
162 WCA. *Wadham College Boat Club Records*, June 1897-99.
163 *The Oxford Mail*, 29th July 1975.
164 St Edmund Hall Archives (SEHA) *The St Edmund Hall Magazine*, 1975-6, pp. 6-7, 'by kind permission of the Principal and Fellows of St Edmund Hall, Oxford'.
165 Keble College Archives (KCA) *The Record*, Keble College 1958
166 Another cook, Bill Jarvis of Magdalen College apparently made an hour-long film of the barges which was unfortunately stolen.
167 Sherwood, Op cit p. 92.
168 *The Hertford College Magazine* 1995-7.
169 *The Hertford College Magazine* May 1911, p. 66.
170 *The Oxford Mail* , May 19th, 1969.
171 M. Maccoun's article 'The Restoration of the Hertford College Barge' *c.* 1967-8, courtesy of Richard Norton.
172 K. Zachariah, Undergraduate Oxford Correspondence. (1912) p. 18. Merton College Zachariah Collection ZAC/2.
173 Ibid. p. 27.
174 Ibid. p. 159 & p. 200.
175 Ibid. p. 199.
176 Ibid. p. 232.
177 Sarah Hosking's article in *Country Life* of January 5th 1967 features the St Catherine's barge.
178 OBC *Captain's Book* 1909-1936.
179 Sherwood, Op. cit. p. 92. Sherwood writes that the Bullingdon Club barge was later known as Loder's barge.
180 Norton writes that The British Queen was in fact the Balliol barge so called by W. H. Black in the *Thames* magazine, April-June 1951.
181 Woodgate, W.B. (1909) p. 185.
182 The Bodleian Library, Dept C. 789: OUBC circular letter, February 13th 1923, vol. 6 (1896-1906).